Withdrawn

Babywearing

The Benefits and Beauty of This Ancient Tradition

By Maria Blois, M.D.

With a Foreword by William Sears, M.D.

Babywearing

The Benefits and Beauty of This Ancient Tradition

© Copyright 2005

Pharmasoft Publishing, L.P.
1712 N. Forest St.
Amarillo, TX   79106-7017
Phone: (806)376-9900
Fax: (806)376-9901
Email: books@ibreastfeeding.com
Website: www.ibreastfeeding.com

ISBN: 0-9729583-3-9

Library of Congress Control Number: 2004116526

To my "sling babies"

Nina

Alanson

TABLE OF CONTENTS

Comparison Charts

Wearing Instructions

Slings

Wraparounds

Front/Back Packs

Torso Carriers

ACKNOWLEDGEMENTS

My heartfelt thanks go to Dr. William Sears for the original inspiration for this book. Hats off to the inventive minds of Rayner Garner and Sachi Yoshimoto, the inventors of the two ringed sling and pioneers of modern babywearing. Mother and babies everywhere - thank you!

For making this project happen, I would like to thank Pharmasoft Publications: Dr. Thomas Hale, my editor - Janet Rourke, and graphic artist - Dolly Moore; Dia Michels for believing in this project from the start; Carole Baas, Ph.D., who has been integral in the development of this book - sending information, ideas, and meticulously editing drafts; Tracy Dower who has shared her time and expertise; and Hilary Flower, my fellow writer, who has been a great source of inspiration and support.

For passing on attached mothers' stories of babywearing, I am indebted to Zan Buckner and Traci Orr. To the women and men who shared their personal stories of babywearing, I say thank you. Thanks also to Elisabeth Ndour for showing me how babies are worn in her part of the world.

I am grateful for my willing photography models: Shelly, Skylar, and Sadie Wilson; Michele and Violet Wiedemer; Alexia and Lydia Louder; Theresa Wohlfeld; Vivian and Fiona Scoggan; Audrey and Eliana Orr; Grace and Harrison Murphy; Gwen and Camille Fancy; Akilah and Memphis Ferguson; Alex and Reed Deines; Siska Blois; Quinn Powers; Claire and Clara Stowell; Margaret Stephenson; Travis Klecka; and Audrey and Toni Dower.

I have been so impressed with the warmth and generosity of the babywearing community. I have over 80 donated carriers in my living room for review in my book. Thank you to Jeni Norton, Barbara Wishingrad, Vesta Garcia, Tanya Westerman, LeAnn Contessa, Susan Gmeiner, Marti Grahl, Darien Wilson, Natasha Walsh, Lisa McDaniel, Julianne Rosado, Jennifer Greenberg, Kristen DeRocha-Powers, Constanze Villines, Nancie Swanke, Sally Nibbelink, Gillian Beerman, Suzanne Shahar, Shelley Aldrich, Angel Gaines, Karen Gonzalez, Joyce Fernandez, Kelley Mason, Lilian Holm-Drumgole, Terrie Abrahamson, Karin Frost, Sally Wilkins, Laney Levine, Jeni Kolstad, Kristine Deppe, Lisa Wood, Annie Lorenzini, Jude Kuipers, Kristi Hayes, Talia Knisley, Stacie Steadman, Amanda Witman, Jody Wright, Stefanie Hollerbach,

Sabrina Sigg, Kaire Downin, and Birgit Marko. Thanks to Rachelle Duvall for her professionalism and her always prompt, courteous help.

Finally, I offer my deepest thanks to my home team: my husband Erik, who went above and beyond to allow me to pursue my passion for babywearing; my children, Nina and Alanson, who were along for the ride (literally!); my father, Richard Giangiulio, for getting me set up with my fabulous camera; my mother, Barbara Loiseau, for the new computer; my sister, Jennifer Fritz, for her enthusiastic support; my brother, Raphi Giangiulio, for letting me work on his computer and posing with his nephew, Kerri Mahar; my in-laws, Elizabeth and Marsden Blois, and Kathryn Blois for reading early drafts and saying this book needed to be written. I am grateful to you all.

The art of babywearing entered the Sears family soon after the birth of our sixth child, Matthew. We regret it took six children to learn the joys of wearing our baby. Martha fabricated a sling out of leftover bedsheet material and we both carried Matthew around in the sling many hours a day. One day Martha happened to mention, "As long as I wear him he's content." Babywearing, that's it! That's what we'll call it. Now we had another Baby B to add to all the other Baby B's of attachment parenting, along with Birth, Bonding, Breastfeeding, Bedding close to baby, and Belief in the signal value of baby's cries.

Shortly thereafter, we met an interesting gentleman from Hawaii, Rayner Garner, who had developed a sliding ring connection to make a sling easy to adjust. This was certainly an improvement over our sling made out of bedsheets. Apparently, Rayner and his wife had been wearing their baby in a sling so he used his engineering background to fabricate this interesting sliding ring apparatus. We bought the ring design from Mr. Garner. Now that we had a prototype sling and ring design to start with, we began experimenting with different sizes and shapes of baby slings and hired a neighbor to start making them in her garage. By coincidence, I had also moved my pediatric practice into a renovated area in our garage so I could be intimately involved with Matthew's growth and development, at least during his first year. (Our patients dubbed my office "Dr. Bill's Garage and Body Shop).

Over the next year, we went through many different shapes and designs for our babysling, trying many of them on our patients. When they came into the office for their first newborn visit, we would give both mom and dad a crash course in babywearing. Soon, I had a whole pediatric practice full of "sling babies." Ah, more material for our books!

We finally settled on a sling shape that worked for most parents most of the time, and our baby sling business outgrew the neighbor's garage. It was time to seek help from a major manufacturer. We chose NoJo because they were a nearby California corporation known for their quality and fashion in infant bedding. It was interesting that the NoJo Corporation (named after the first two children of the two mothers who started the corporation, Noelle and Joanna) also began as a home business making bedding supplies in their garages.

Babywearing is not a new concept and certainly we did not "invent" the sling. For centuries mothers all over the world have been wearing their babies in various types of slings. Yet, Martha and I wanted to bring the ancient art of babywearing into Western cultures. We felt it belonged in the whole package of the high-touch style of attachment parenting since, because of the fear of spoiling, the predominant parenting styles at that time were those of low-touch parenting.

I once attended an international parenting conference while I was wearing our seventh baby, Stephen, in the NoJo sling we called "The Original Babysling." I noticed there were many other mothers, many from third-world countries, also wearing their babies in slings made out of fabric that matched their native dress. One evening I asked two mothers from Zambia, "Why do you carry your babies in slings?" I received two simple, yet profound answers: "It does good things for babies" and "It makes life easier for parents." In a nutshell, that's what babywearing does.

My confession: I use our family and pediatric office as a sort of laboratory to study what parenting styles work best, and that's where Martha and I get most of the material for our books. Our books really are written on the job. So, over the next twenty years, I studied the sling babies in our family and pediatric practice, and here are the benefits of babywearing I discovered:

Sling babies thrive. After years of watching a whole parade of babywearers in our pediatric practice, we noticed that these babies thrive. Thriving means more than just getting taller and heavier. Thriving means growing optimally – physically, emotionally, and intellectually.

Sling babies are calmer. You can say that familiarity breeds content. The motion and closeness to a familiar caregiver puts baby in a state of quiet alertness, the behavioral state in which babies are most content. We believe this is because babywearing duplicates the womb environment. Their legs and arms are contained because there's no room to fling them out. They hear mother's heartbeat, feel her breathing, and are rocked by the gentle motions of her body – the organizing and calming rhythm that baby was used to in the womb.

Contrast this with crib and playpen babies. These babies fuss more and develop purposeless, jerky movements or self-rocking behaviors that are signs of disorganization. These "behind-bars" babies often waste a lot of energy that they could have used for thriving.

Babywearing is especially helpful for high-need babies, those whom we nickname "More." It is also very helpful in those early months for "p.m. fussers" who save up all their energy for a long blast of crying in the late afternoon or early evening. We would plan ahead for this "happy hour" and wear our baby for a long walk in the sling. The fresh air and motion would calm our baby and, as a perk, we would get some exercise.

Sling babies are smarter. If babies spend less time crying, what do they do with their free time? They learn! Sling babies spend more time in the state of quiet alertness, the behavioral state in which baby is most interested in interacting with his environment. Baby learns a lot in the arms of a busy caregiver. When worn in a sling, baby is intimately involved in the world of the wearer. Baby hears what mother or father hears and sees what they see. When Matthew was nine months of age, as soon as I would mention the cue word "go!," he would crawl over to the door and look up at the sling hanging on a hook nearby. He knew that he would soon be in my arms and in my world.

Babywearing makes daycare easier. For parents who need to have their baby in daycare, I write them a prescription that says, "For medical reasons, please wear this baby at least three hours a day." Then I advise mothers to play show and tell with their caregiver. Show the caregiver how to wear baby in whatever carrier baby has become used to, and tell her why it's so important.

Work and wear. When Martha was a lactation consultant and taught breastfeeding classes, if Matthew was going through a high-need period, she would frequently wear him during a class. One day after she gave a talk on attachment parenting to 150 pediatricians, some of the doctors came up to her afterwards and said, "What you did made more of an impression than what you said." Many mothers in our practice have the type of jobs that allow them to wear their babies while they work. Even a couple of receptionists in our office wore their babies to work for a few months.

One of our most memorable babywearing moments was when we were invited to a black-tie formal affair when our son Stephen was two months old. Stephen was born with Down Syndrome and we knew that babywearing was doubly important for his development. Rather than decline the invitation, Martha had a babysling made to match her formal gown. We called this "formal babywear." I'll never forget the expression on some of the guests' faces when we walked into the party wearing Stephen. You could almost read their minds, wondering, "What's that she's wearing?" When they saw how content Stephen was and how natural the formal-wearing scene was to us, the previously raised eyebrows changed to social admiration.

Another memorable experience was when Martha wore one-year-old Stephen during a one-hour interview on "The Donahue Show." Stephen was contained and content as he nursed and slept through the whole show as a witness to the world that the ancient art of babywearing was returning to our culture.

Twenty years later we are still experiencing the joys of having sling babies – and sling grandbabies – in our family and in our pediatric practice. Martha and I applaud Dr. Blois for showing in this book that there are many ways to wear a baby. If your babies could talk, they would ask you to please read this book and wear them as often as possible. Raise a sling baby. It's a wonderful way to get to know your baby.

-- William and Martha Sears

Introduction

New M.D., New Mom

I graduated from medical school and gave birth to our first child two months later. I quickly discovered that my training as a physician had prepared me to deal with illness and injury, but in beginning my mothering journey, I felt very unprepared for normal, healthy babyhood. I was also unprepared for how isolating mothering can feel.

In my pre-children days, as part of my medical school training, I was given a pager and sent to rotate with a surgical team at a big, county hospital. Every third night, my team was "on-call" meaning we would get paged if any patient required services of a surgical nature. That first night, I sat awake in the on-call room watching my pager, waiting for it to go off. I slept fitfully. I felt wired. I felt like I had little control over my own time. I was often called out of bed to tend to someone whose needs were greater than my own. It was always such a relief to turn off that pager.

Flash forward two years: After my first night at home with my own newborn daughter, I sit awake watching her sleep. It has been a long night. She has nursed many times and seems to wake up just as I doze off. My mind drifts back to that on-call room, and I am struck by the uncanny similarity of the two situations. I am not getting much sleep, I feel wired and out of control, and I have to take care of someone else's needs instead of my own.

There are some key differences, however. After being "on-call" with my infant all night, I get none of the social approval that I enjoyed while I was a med student. No one tells me how interesting my work is and how lucky I am to be pursuing this particular path. I have no "classmates" to complain to over breakfast. No one asks for details. No one is even interested, quite frankly. And most importantly, this time I have no way to turn off my "pager" the next day or night.

My discovery? Mothering is hard work! We mothers want the best for our children. There are no shortcuts, and there is often no visible way to measure our success. It is not so singularly difficult. There is not one task that is awful. It is simply that parenting is *relentless*. Infants require tending even when we are ill, tired, angry or bored. We get no vacations, no sick days, no lunch breaks. I'm on call 24 hours a day, seven days a week. There is no way to turn parenting off, nor do we want to. I have found parenting to be a very humbling journey. We get back what we invest in our children.

During my pregnancy, I felt peaceful and confident. I had always loved babies and children. My Nana predicted that I would have seven of my own when I was just a little girl. I would be a natural… No problem. Now four years and two babies later, I am much wiser, less confident perhaps, but certainly thriving. I understand now that there is no such thing as a "natural" mother. We all work very hard. Mothering is hands down the hardest job I have ever had, and mind you, I have worked nights at a county emergency room.

As a mother, I am interested in doing what is best for my own children, and as a physician, I am interested in studying what works well for other children. This is the story of how I discovered the soothing peace of babywearing with my own babies, and how I have attempted to apply this knowledge to help babies everywhere. Anything (such as babywearing) that is clearly good for babies and makes parenting more of a pleasure for both adults and babies has my full support.

Beyond the Bjorn[a]

I came upon my first sling quite by accident. My first baby was two weeks old, and I was shopping in a fancy baby boutique. I came across a sling display. I was mildly curious, but mostly skeptical. The sling looked very flimsy and complicated. The kind saleslady arranged it over my shoulder and showed me how to slip my newborn into the carrier. My daughter promptly nestled down and went to sleep with a sigh of contentment. I was stunned. I felt an enormous sense of freedom and did not quite seem to know what to do with my suddenly unencumbered hands. My heart skipped a beat as I looked lovingly at my nestled babe. All was peaceful. I immediately bought the sling. I finished shopping and walked to another store. My baby slept contently for the next three hours until it was time to nurse again. I felt like I was on to something BIG here.

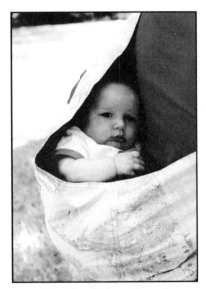

Babies love slings!

I went home and showed my new purchase to my husband. He listened politely to my excited story and then went on about his business. I used my new sling happily throughout the next few days. Chores around the house were much easier. I started being able to cook meals again and felt a little bit more in control. Magically, my baby seemed more content and appeared to sleep and nurse better. She just seemed like a happy little girl. People would comment on how content she looked and how I was so "lucky" to have such an easy baby. My husband noticed the changes and was soon a sling enthusiast himself, reaching for it each time he went out to do yard work or we went for a walk together.

[a] *The Baby Bjorn is a popular front pack carrier that is sold in many major baby stores and leading baby product catalogs. Currently, it seems to be the carrier that many new parents end up trying.*

The public response to the sling was profound. People would stop me in the streets and pepper me with questions: *Did you make that? Your baby looks so content, where did you get that? Where can I find one? I had a sling, but I could never figure the darn thing out*, they would tell me. I found myself doing impromptu demonstrations in parking lots and writing sling information on scraps of paper for all these parents. When I carried my two-month old daughter in the sling at a wedding, another guest approached me and said:

> *I have been a pediatrician for the past 35 years and I have never seen such a content little baby. I have been watching you all evening and your baby never fusses! I am going to recommend this sling to all my patients.*

Despite such positive reviews, I never saw other babies in slings. All around me, babies were being pushed in strollers and carriages. After that initial boutique, I never even saw similar slings for sale. I felt like the sole sling user in the world. I was mystified. Why was such a wonderful contraption for both mother and baby so hard to come by? Why didn't every new mama have a sling? How in the world did people get by without one? Everyone seemed to own a front pack and had never even heard of a sling. Although front packs can certainly work for some people, they did not seem to have the versatility or longevity of other methods of carrying baby. Why weren't other options more well-known?

Then I went to my first La Leche League meeting, a national organization that offers information, encouragement, and support for women who choose to breastfeed. I walked in and saw slings and contented babies everywhere. I slowly began to learn about slings in general and other even less known ways of carrying babies close, such as wraparound carriers and front/back packs. As my daughter got older, I began carrying her on my back with a wraparound carrier. Again, I was bombarded with questions: *How did you get her on your back? Where can I get a similar carrier?*

I became fascinated with the many types of carriers that exist. While learning more about the types of devices that carry our babies, I stumbled upon a vast store of medical literature supporting the idea of keeping baby close. As it turns out, ***wearing our babies in a soft carrier does them a world of good***, besides just making our lives as parents easier. Premature babies, especially, seem to benefit from being held constantly close to mother's body in what is known as "kangaroo care." I was excited by this information and wanted to apply it to my life for both my babies and the babies of friends and family. I felt there was a lack of information and support for this great parenting tool that is babywearing.

I decided a book was needed that celebrated the wonderful benefits of babywearing, referencing both medically-based research and anecdotal evidence. With my background as both a physician (well-versed in child development, physiology, and anatomy) and a babywearing mother, I felt I was uniquely qualified to address some of the most frequently asked questions concerning babywearing (i.e. behavioral and developmental issues). I wanted to present solid medical evidence that babywearing is good for parents and babies in addition to the convenience aspects. I also wanted to include detailed step-by-step (non-intimidating) instructions for wearing baby. I planned to catalogue the rich variety of available baby carriers, including numerous examples of babywearing in real life with plenty of beautiful photos of happy babies being carried by a variety of caregivers.

With this book, I hope to contribute to the growing body of literature that *values the parent-child attachment and envisions ours as a baby-friendly world.*

In this book, you will:

- Learn how wearing your baby can make your baby more content, sleep better, learn better, and cry less.
- Hear from experienced babywearers from all over the country.
- Learn how to choose and use the carrier that is right for you.

Part 1:

Choosing to
Wear Your Baby

Why should you wear your baby? In this section, we will see that there are many great reasons to wear your baby, both for you and for your baby, but it all boils down to this:

Wear your baby and you can enjoy a brighter, better behaved baby. Life can be sweeter for both of you.

Chapter 1

The Benefits of Babywearing

Babies love to be carried. Every day, all over the world, babies lift up their arms to loved ones in the universal language that means: *Pick me up, please.* One of my daughter's first sentences was "Mommy, hole choo!" which she said as she held both arms out to me in a precious plea. I assume she was parroting what I usually said when she motioned to be picked up: "Do you want Mommy to hold you?" Our babies are clever. They are born knowing how to signal their biological needs - they root when they need to nurse, they smile when they need vital eye contact for optimal brain development, they cling to our fingers and our clothing in an effort to stay close, and they love being held. There is a good biological reason for these behaviors: they help babies survive and thrive. There are many emotional and physical benefits to holding baby close.

Babywearing is Good for Babies

Biologically, babies *need* to be carried in order to thrive. Studies have shown that otherwise well nourished and cared for infants who are deprived of human touch fail to thrive and can even die. Good things happen when baby is carried. Research shows that babies who are held often:

- **cry less:** Studies have shown that the more babies are held, the less they cry.[1,2] The long-term consequences of letting infants cry without responding are just beginning to be understood. One study found that letting babies cry permanently alters the nervous system by flooding the developing brain with stress hormones. This makes these babies overly sensitive to future trauma and may lead to incidents of post-traumatic stress and panic disorders in adulthood.[3] Babies who cry less in the first few months cry less in the following year.[4] Responding quickly to your crying baby is an investment – the less she cries now the more peaceful the upcoming year. It is well worth your effort.

- **are more calm and content:** Carried babies have a more regular respiratory rate, heart rate, and steady internal body temperature. Even very tiny premature babies can be carried safely in a sling without danger of compromised breathing or heart rate.[5] Regularly carrying a baby encourages baby to feel secure and content.

- **sleep more peacefully:** Keeping baby close helps baby organize his sleep/ wake cycles. Naptimes are spent in constant motion, close to mother's heart and night time is dark and still with a loved parent nearby. This helps baby know the difference between daytime and nighttime, an important step in sleeping longer stretches at night. One study of premature infants found that babies had longer intervals of quiet sleep when they had skin-to-skin contact with mother.[6]

- **nurse better, gain weight better:** Research has shown that premature babies who are touched and held gain weight faster and are healthier than babies who are not.[7,8] Full-term babies nurse more frequently when they are carried close to mother.[9]

- **enjoy better digestion:** The constant motion and frequent small feedings associated with carrying baby can promote good digestion. Babies who are carried often spit up less. Babies with gastroesophageal reflux disease (GERD)[b] can benefit from being carried in the upright position after a feeding. When baby is upright, the force of gravity helps the acid stay down in the stomach where it belongs. Most babies outgrow this condition.

> Bridgette has problems with reflux. While very rare in breastfed babies, it still occurs. She has a mild case, and by being creative, we have been able to manage difficulties without medication. We found that anytime she was in a reclined, flat position she would be in pain. The sling, for us, was a wonderful solution - a way to keep her upright, free of pain and medication.
>
> Bradi, Virginia

> Arden (3½ months old) was diagnosed with GERD when she was a month old. Often mistaken for extreme colic, this has left her in pain each time she feeds. The only way I can help my baby calm down and feed properly is to wear her as much as possible. I not only feed her in a sling, but I carry her almost all hours of the day. This has helped her to sleep and eat well. She is now a healthy 15 pounds and loves being held.
>
> Catherine, Ontario, Canada

- **develop better:** Babies who are held experience human touch and movement. This stimulation has been shown to have a positive effect on the baby's development.[10] Carrying baby enhances motor skills by stimulating the vestibular system (used for balance). Baby constantly readjusts as mother moves around, using his developing muscles to hold his head up, kick his feet and use his arms to cling to mother. Because soft carriers keep pressure off the back of the head, carried babies are at a much lower risk for plagiocephaly (asymmetrical head shape). Carrying baby naturally limits the time baby spends in hard plastic carriers, such as carseats, automatic swings, and such. Holding baby while moving counts as "tummy time."[c]

[b] *Gastroesophageal reflux disease (GERD) is a common newborn condition in which acid from the stomach refluxes back up through the not quite competent esophageal sphincter causing a burning sensation.*

[c] *"Tummy time" refers to placing baby on her stomach when she's awake and being observed. It is thought that several 5 to 10 minute periods a day of tummy time will help baby with balance and strengthen the upper body muscles that are later used for sitting and crawling.*

Carrying utilizes and supports the way a baby develops control of his body from the head down. A carried baby is better equipped for the next stages of motor development, and there is no need for exercises or forced tummy time. Excess energy is discharged, and there is less tension and discontent.

Lilian Holm-Drumgole
Physical Therapist, Developer of the Baby Back-Tie Carrier

There are other physical advantages of being carried for baby. Babywearing can be kind to baby's developing hip joints. Baby hips are unique in that formation is not complete at birth. The acetabulum is the area of the pelvis that is capable of becoming a hip socket. The proximal head of the femur (the thigh bone) fits into the acetabulum and forms the ball-and-socket joint of the hip. In newborns, this area is cartilage, and as the child matures, this area will ossify or harden into bone. When baby straddles our front or our back, his legs are said to be *flexed* (knees pulled up towards head) and *abducted* (knees away from midline). This position places the head of the femur directly against the acetabulum and encourages deepening of the socket which promotes healthy hip development. In fact, children with hip dysplasia are often placed in this position to help correct the problem.[11]

Hip dysplasia occurs when the top of the femur is not properly located in the hip socket. It can be congenital (present at birth) or developmental.[12] The primary cause of hip dysplasia is thought to be genetic. The way we carry our babies will not *prevent* genetically susceptible children from developing hip dysplasia.[13,14] We may, however, be able to promote healthy hip development in borderline cases. In short, carrying baby in the flexed, abducted position is good for the hip development of *all* babies and may be especially important for those who are mildly genetically predisposed to developing hip dysplasia.

Babies who are carried have a good vantage point from which to observe life. The movement helps baby feel that he is *in* life not just observing life. When we carry our babies, we can interact with them more readily.

People often make eye contact and speak to baby which can promote greater visual alertness and language development.

What is Babywearing?

Babies need to be carried, but, goodness, our arms can get tired! Soft carriers can help. Around the world, babies are carried in cloth carriers near the human body. These can be slings, pouches, packs or wraparound carriers. Renowned pediatrician, Dr. William Sears, coined the phrase *babywearing,[d]* which simply refers to carrying your baby in a soft carrier close to your body as you go about the daily business of your life.

He suggests that we make carried babies the norm and that we watch for cues as to when baby wants to be put down.[15] This is a reversal of the more culturally prevalent idea of babies lying passively in a variety of baby holders such as carseats, bouncy seats, swings, and strollers, watching while we go about our daily activities. Take baby along! We have taken our babies in a sling to weddings, restaurants, movies, parties, professional conferences, and the beach. It is a bit like having a stroller folded up

"Care for some tea?"
We interact with our
carried babies!

in the diaper bag. Babies love being in a soft carrier and will usually watch contentedly from their perch or even go right to sleep.

> I can't imagine parenting without a sling! They embody everything that is warm, cozy, snuggly, loving and wonderful about parenting. They truly seem like a part of your body- the pouch that we were unfortunately born without. If I have to come back as an animal next time, I hope it's a kangaroo!
>
> Molly, Washington

[d] *The terms "babywearing" and "wear your baby" are trademarked and are used throughout the text of this book with the permission of Dr. William Sears.*

Reclaiming an Ancient Tradition

We tend to think of babywearing as an innovative new idea, a thoroughly modern choice, but it has actually been around for quite a while. As a man in the airport once commented when he noticed my sling and asked me if I had ever traveled to Africa, "At home, women have been carrying babies like that for *centuries*."

We human beings have always been ingenious at finding ways to strap our babies to our bodies. Many cultures have their own distinct traditional way of carrying babies. Some cultures use a simple piece of cloth to secure baby to the caregiver. The Mexican *rebozo* (shawl), the African *kanga* or *kikoy* (rectangular piece of fabric), the Indonesian *selendang* or *sarong* (long strip of cloth wrapped around the body, also worn as a skirt or dress), the Peruvian *manta* (square blanket), the Tahitian *pareo* (rectangular piece of printed cotton cloth also used as a wraparound skirt), and the South Asian *sari* or *saree* (several yards of lightweight cloth draped so that one end forms a skirt and the other end goes over the head or shoulder) are all examples of indigenous cloth baby carriers. Some cultures have developed a slightly more constructed method for carrying baby, such as the Chinese *mei tai* strap back carrier, the Korean *podaegi* (a blanket with straps that is used as a back carrier), and the *onbuhimo* Japanese tie-on pack. Babywearing is so common in these cultures that its presence in everyday life is illustrated in the indigenous artwork of these areas.

Mother and child
(Mexico)

Mother and child
(Senegal)

Promoting in-arms parenting has been my passion since I first saw traditional babywearing come alive on the buses, back roads, street corners, and markets of southern Mexico and Guatemala as I watched babies being carried in *rebozos* and *sutes* (native shawls and cloths). The women moved with grace and dignity; the babies moved with them, wide-eyed, alert, and mostly quiet. The moms were out and about, laughing, socializing, shopping, and working with both hands free! I confirmed this experience with my own two sons: babywearing was our safe place, our key to fun, contentment, and nurturing. Nothing else has made quite the same impact in my parenting.

Barbara Wishingrad
Founder and President of the Rebozo Way Project
Non-profit dedicated to encouraging in-arms parenting

I have always been amazed as I traveled extensively throughout the Third World where babywearing is such a part of everyday life, how in the market, on buses, everywhere, babies are *completely content*. You virtually never hear a baby crying in such places. It is the exception to hear babies cry. You don't realize that no baby cries until you do hear a baby cry, and you are *surprised* by the stark contrast of the sound.

Erik, Texas

Somehow, somewhere modern industrial society "lost" our ancient wisdom and traditions regarding babywearing. There are probably many complex reasons for this transition. Industrialization and frequent physical separation of mother and baby, the invention and frequent use of strollers, strong Western values of early "independence," the shift from extended families being the norm to the smaller nuclear family that is common today all interfere with the basic mother/baby relationship and cause that relationship to suffer. We may never know all the reasons we strayed from wearing our babies, but it is time to reclaim it for our children. Babies need to be held close and babywearing is a wonderful, practical, *developmentally sound* way to meet our babies' needs as well as our own.

Holding a baby with a simple piece of cloth is a beautiful, ancient art that belongs to all of humanity. It must not be lost. Learn it. Then teach everyone you know.

Tracy Dower
Creator of The Mamatoto Project, Inc.
Non-profit promoting babywearing

Sacagawea and child

The History of Babywearing in the U.S.[e]

The first Americans to wear their babies were the Native Americans who carried their babies (papooses) in cradle boards and cloth carriers mainly on their backs. This tradition was widespread among the Native people throughout the area that is now the United States. In fact, the image of a Native American woman carrying her child on her back – a woman known as Sacagawea – is engraved on the United States gold one dollar coin.

Origins of the Two Ringed Sling

The two ringed sling was invented on the island of Hawaii in 1981 by Rayner Garner for his daughter, Fonda. Rayner and his wife, Sachi, had read *The Contiuum Concept* by Jean Liedloff and were inspired to carry their baby. They tried to carry newborn Fonda in a front pack, but she developed a heat rash. Frustrated with the front pack, Rayner reached into his closet and pulled out a wool scarf, knotted it, slung it over his shoulder, and put Fonda in it. She gave a soft sigh, curled up, and promptly went to sleep. This way of carrying was a revelation to Sachi. She says: "In the sling, Fonda was cradled in a natural position and nursing her was so easy to do. We both felt close, cool, and happy."

Sachi and baby Fonda
Their first knotted sling - April 1981
(Used with permission)

[e] *Based on a series of phone interviews with Rayner Garner, Sachi Yoshimoto, and Dr. William Sears, September, 2004.*

The knotted scarf was fine for the first few days, but they soon discovered that it was difficult to adjust. Rayner is tall and Sachi is short. They had to constantly retie the knot each time they took turns or each time Sachi wanted to nurse the baby. Putting his inventive mind to work, Rayner attempted to devise a method for quickly adjusting the fabric without compromising safety. The method needed to "jam" the fabric and keep it from slipping with the weight of the baby. Rayner had a vision of seeing that sort of design on a boat and decided to try a two ringed design.

Rayner and Fonda
First two ringed sling - 1981
(Used with permission)

He took a piece of cotton fabric 36 inches wide and sewed two wooden curtain rings on one end and folded the other end "like a paper airplane," ending up with a two-inch tail which he threaded through the rings. This simple innovation made the sling remarkably easy to adjust. He added a shoulder pad and eventually side rail padding, at Sachi's suggestion, when Fonda was six months old and started riding in the hip carry. The shoulder pad end was made with the ability to add further padding if it became necessary. They deliberately chose beautiful fabrics because, from the beginning, they felt that the slings needed to be fashionable as well as practical in order to have an impact on our "image conscious culture." They experimented with various fabrics for different needs, such as silk slings for formal occasions and net water slings.

Rayner and his family made an enormous contribution to modern babywearing. He gave the simple indigenous cloth sling form and shape. Rayner's basic sling design gives the modern parent many of the same benefits of the indigenous sling – the simplicity of use (easy on and off), ease of nursing, natural support for holding positions, versatility of holding positions, and easy transitions between holding positions. As Sachi notes: "Rayner's two ringed tailored sling is, in essence, a bridge between the indigenous cloth sling and the highly constructed baby carriers of modern society (strollers, framed backpacks, and such)." He created a comfortable and practical sling for the modern day parent. His basic design (and Rayner and Sachi's vision of the sling as a fashion accessory for the nurturing parent) continues to be the inspiration and the functional springboard for the development of countless other baby sling models nationwide.

Popularizing Babywearing

In 1985, Dr. William Sears and his wife, Martha, welcomed their sixth child, Matthew, to the world. As they thought he was going to be their last child, they were determined to proceed through the early years with great deliberation, taking care to enjoy and notice each stage. They began carrying Matthew everywhere and used baby sheets to tie him to their body for convenience. Dr. Sears eventually tried Rayner Garner's pre-fabricated baby sling fashioned with two rings. Dr. Sears was impressed with the practicality of the design and bought the design rights in order to reproduce the slings.[f]

Using tied sheet to carry Matthew
(Used with permission)

Dr. Sears made his slings under the trademarked name of *The Original BabySling* in his garage and in the garages of neighboring stay-at-home moms. The idea was a hit. Although babywearing was by no means a new phenomenon (people have been wearing their babies in many cultures for hundreds of years), Dr. Sears was instrumental in popularizing the idea of babywearing in the U.S.

Over time, Dr. Sears modified Rayner Garner's original sling design. He added teeth to the marine quality nylon rings to prevent the fabric from slipping through the rings, and he added a bar stopper at the end of the sling. Since the debut of *The Original BabySling*, many other slings have popped up on the market, some with remarkably similar designs and some with slight variations.

[f] *Rayner Garner retained the right to compete with his latest design. He and Sachi consulted with other sling companies and refined their own line of slings. A few years ago, Sachi started a custom-made service which she named EnWrapture. Rayner went on to create a number of slings that have a specialized application.*

Dr. Sears clearly considers imitation a form of flattery saying: "I'm delighted there are so many slings." One of his main goals is to promote babywearing as an attachment tool that helps babies get connected. He contends that babywearing duplicates the womb and "does good things for babies." Babywearing clearly fits his motto of supporting the things that are good for babies and that make life easier for parents.

Soft baby carriers have enjoyed a resurgence of popularity since being "rediscovered" in the mid 1980s.

Carrying Matthew in The Original BabySling

(Used with permission)

There has been a real explosion in the number of new brands and even types of soft baby carriers available over the last few years, although you would never realize it if you shopped only in retail stores. Most of the excellent new products available are made by work-at-home mothers and sold over the Internet. The customer service is outstanding and some slings are so popular that they have waiting lists of a month or more.

Jennifer Norton
Creator of *TheBabyWearer.com*
On-line Babywearing Resource Center

More and more parents from all walks of life are trying out the babywearing lifestyle. Celebrities such as Brooke Shields, Cindy Crawford, Kate Hudson, Courteney Cox-Arquette and Gwyneth Paltrow have all been recently spotted wearing their babies. (See www.mammasmilk.com for the great "Celebrity Slingers" photo gallery).

Once we get used to our soft baby carriers, we often feel lost without them. They quickly become our most valued piece of baby equipment.

The sling is the absolute only item I have NEVER packed away between children. I love, love, love it! It is my standard baby shower gift.

Jennifer, Ohio

I love my sling! Of all the baby 'paraphernalia' we have bought, the sling has become our most prized possession. While other 'must have' items have sat around collecting dust, our sling has been collecting memories.

Christine, New Jersey

Babywearing Enhances Parent-Baby Bonding

Babywearing has the potential to revolutionize parenting in Western nations. Just consider how fulfilling parenting could be with a happy baby *and* two free hands.

Jennifer Norton
Creator of *TheBabyWearer.com*
On-line Babywearing Resource Center

Science is just catching up and telling us what babies have always known: holding babies is good for babies. Keeping babies close can make us more responsive parents. One study found that mothers who were given soft carriers at birth were more responsive to their three-month-old babies and the babies were more securely attached.[16] Another study found that frequent skin-to-skin contact between mothers and their premature babies helped the mothers become better at detecting and responding to infant cues.[17] Babies with responsive parents cry less.[18] This is good news for everyone involved. More importantly, we now understand that parental responsiveness to baby is a crucially important factor in optimal brain development. When a baby signals a need and parents respond, the behavior is reinforced and takes on meaning.

When a mother is perceptive to her child's signals and responds promptly and appropriately to them, her child thrives and the relationship develops happily.

A question that is constantly raised both by mothers and professionals is whether it is wise for a mother always to meet her child's demands for her presence and attention. Will giving in to him lead to his becoming 'spoilt'? The question is perhaps best seen in the same perspective as the question: 'How much food is good for a child?' From the earliest months forward, it is best to follow a child's lead. A child is so made that, if left to decide, he can regulate his own food intake. Therefore, a mother can safely leave the initiative to him.

The same is true of attachment behavior, especially during the early years. In an ordinary family in which a mother is caring for her child, no harm comes to him when she gives him as much of her presence and attention as he seems to want. Thus, in regard to mothering – as to food – a young child seems to be so made that, if from the first he is permitted to decide, he can satisfactorily regulate his own 'intake.'

From *Attachment* by John Bowlby[19]

Babywearing can help us care for our child in a way that can bring out the best in baby.

> As a young father and psychiatrist, babywearing has intuitively made so much sense to me in terms of helping my infant develop basic trust. Actually, I would even say that basic trust does not need to be learned. It is our natural way of being from birth. Babies actually develop *mistrust* by not being held and by being physically isolated, particularly in the first year of life. Babywearing has been so important to my relationship with my daughter and later, my son. Every moment I held her, I felt I was giving her the gift of basic trust.
>
> Erik Blois, MD
> Psychiatrist and father of two

Mothers who wear their babies often report feeling a comforting sense of closeness to their baby. They are able to fully enjoy the sights and smells of their little ones nestled close to their body.

> If your baby is always in a stroller or car seat, how do you get to smell them? My daughter has the most wonderful-smelling head. My husband thinks I'm a little wacky (he calls me 'very smell-oriented'), but I just can't get enough of her smell.
>
> Sharon, Colorado

Babywearing is Practical

Why do I wear my baby? Quite frankly, because my arm gets tired. We are already holding our babies, we might as well slip a sling under their bum to make our load easier. I always get asked if my back hurts while using a specific carrier. There seems to be the idea that with the "perfect carrier" baby will not feel heavy, and we will not get tired carrying him. One thing to remember is that we start carrying our babies when they are very small, and as they grow, so does our strength. By the time baby is 20 pounds, we have grown accustomed to carrying a heavier and heavier baby. Alas, there is no perfect carrier. All carriers have their pluses and their minuses: the trick is to find the carrier that best meets your needs. Carriers do not make our backs hurt, our heavy babies do. Carriers offer relief!

I had to laugh when my father-in-law had his blinding moment of insight. On a recent visit to my in-laws, our one-year-old son developed a strong attachment to his grandfather and wanted to be in his arms at all times. Granddad was tickled to be so popular, but had never considered the toll it could take. One evening he was trying to clean up the kitchen and get dinner started and Alanson insisted on being in his arms, howling indignantly each time Granddad tried to set him down. After several false starts, he finally consigned himself to working one-handed. He laughed and said: "Ah-ha, I see the need for Maria's book now! How do you get anything done with a one-year-old who always wants to be held?" He finished up his work and said with a twinkle in his eye: "I could be the "before" picture for your "Before and After Using a Baby Carrier" section with my sore back and tired arm with the caption: *Warning, this could happen to you! Purchase and use your baby carrier NOW.*"

There is a beauty and simplicity in keeping baby close. I have found my sling especially handy when we travel. Several years ago, we took our then two-month-old daughter to France. She stayed in the sling throughout busy airports, crowded buses, noisy trains, and sightseeing. I always had a free hand to help with luggage, and I was glad to keep her close. She was a pleasure the whole trip, and I certainly credit my sling.

More recently, I traveled alone across country with my two children. At one point, our flight was delayed several hours. The baby needed a nap and the toddler was hungry and needed to find a potty. I thought fast. I nursed the baby and then tied him to my back with my tie sling. With him firmly in place, we went and found a potty for the toddler. I then put her in the stroller with a snack. I walked around the airport until the baby fell asleep on my back, pushing the stroller with the munching toddler in front of me. When it was time to board the flight, I slid the baby back around to the front. He slept on and on. In fact, he ended up sleeping most of the flight in the sling, and the trip was a big success. The flight attendant passed by numerous times to peek at the sleeping baby and remarked that it was such a pleasure to see a baby so contented on a flight. The sling helped me meet both my children's needs even in extenuating circumstances.

Baby carriers can be invaluable in many other ways. Soft baby carriers can be a great way to bring your baby along to social events where babies are not usually content.

My husband's and my family both live out of state, and we are fortunate to be able to visit them fairly often. Our son (now 15 months) sleeps peacefully in the sling for hours in the middle of dinner parties and other loud family gatherings. If it wasn't for the sling, either he wouldn't have slept and been really cranky or we wouldn't have been able to spend so much time with our families while visiting.

Tiffiny, Arizona

Babies held close to mama seldom are any trouble. It is easy to put a sleeping baby down for a nap in a soft baby carrier. Simply bend over and put baby down on the bed, leave the carrier in place behind baby, slip the carrier over your head, and tiptoe away. Because the soft carrier smells like home, leaving the carrier tucked around baby often confers a sense of tranquility that can help baby sleep better. One time when I was photographing a mother-baby pair, baby Toni fell asleep in her sling. Her mother laid her gently next to her ten-year-old sister, still wrapped up in the carrier, and she slept soundly the rest of the afternoon.

With a second child, a baby carrier is very useful for outings to the park and such. This leaves you with one baby in the carrier and a free hand for the older sibling.

Baby carriers feel like home

Babywearing allows us to get back to doing the things that we love to do. We enjoy a very active lifestyle with our daughter, Tessa, and our three horses. Thanks to babywearing, she has been riding with me since she was seven weeks old. I would put her in her pouch, and we would go off on rides. She would almost always fall asleep in the saddle. Now at two, she still rides with me, but she is big enough to sit in the saddle by herself. I have to say that I miss the days of carrying my baby close, but I know she will always be close to my heart. We share a special bond that only a mother and child can share, and I am sure it was strengthened by keeping her so close from the very beginning.

Jeannette, North Dakota

Babywearing Facilitates Breastfeeding

Biologically, the fat content and calories in breastmilk *require* a newborn to nurse often, a minimum of eight to twelve times in each 24 hour period. A newborn must nurse this often in order to get the fat and calories she needs to grow and develop.

In a book published in 1972,[20] Nicolas Blurton Jones divided mothers in the animal kingdom into two basic types: *continuous feeders* and *spaced feeders*. Continuous feeders are defined as mothers who carry or are followed by their young and are, therefore, in constant contact with them. *Spaced feeders* are mothers who cache their young or keep them in nests. According to Blurton Jones, continuous feeders feed their young more or less continuously, and their milk is low in fat and protein. Also, their infants suckle slowly. Spaced feeders, on the other hand, feed their young at widely spaced intervals, and their milk has a high protein and fat content. Their infants suckle at a fast rate.

Analysis of human milk has definitively shown that we fall into the category of continuous feeders.

> With a fat content of 4.2% and a protein content of 0.9%, human milk clearly puts us in the category of *continuous feeders*. This fits in well with what we know of infant care in the few remaining hunter-gatherer societies, the Kung of the Kalahari Desert and the Papua New Guineans, whose mothers carry their infants (on their hips or in a sling) and nurse them very frequently (during the day as often as every fifteen minutes, and at night at least once until they are about three years old). It also makes sense of some of the idiosyncrasies of the modern human's behavior, such as the fact that a crying baby is quieted by rocking movements in the range of sixty cycles per minute, just the speed of a human female as she walks slowly, looking for food perhaps, and carrying an infant on her hip. Or the fact that today's infant is noisy, in sharp contrast to the silence of most primate babies. The wailing that we've come to expect from our infants may not always have been part of their behavior pattern. Infants who are in constant skin-to-skin contact with their mothers rarely get so hungry that they cry for food. Their mothers are able to read their early hunger signals – moving, gurgling, fretting – and help their infants to the breast long before they get to the point of crying.
>
> From *A Natural History of Parenting* by Susan Allport[21]

With the amount of time a newborn baby needs to spend nursing, it makes sense to keep baby close with a soft carrier – otherwise a breastfeeding mother may find it difficult to do much other than sit and nurse her newborn. Breastfeeding in a soft carrier is easy and discreet. Baby is already near the food source and mother just pulls the fabric out of the way and allows the baby free access. There is no need to stop or sit down. Special clothes with nursing openings can make this process even more streamlined (for example, Motherwear Catalog www.motherwear.com, 1-800-950-2500). Some types of soft carriers have extra fabric that may be draped strategically to completely cover the action (for example, the tail of an open-tailed sling).

The ability to breastfeed baby in a carrier may not seem important, but as any new breastfeeding mother knows, being able to breastfeed with baby still in the carrier is crucial. Tiny babies nurse a lot; in fact, sometimes it can seem non-stop. Often baby just gets settled in the carrier and it is time to nurse again. It can be exhausting to get baby back out again and get resettled to nurse.

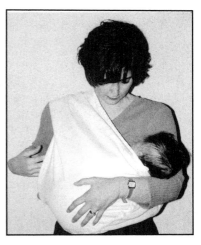

Breastfeeding discreetly in a sling

I remember one time, when my firstborn was a few months old, we were on a long train ride and she was sleeping peacefully in the sling. She started squirming and squeaking, and I knew she was starting to get hungry. I looked anxiously around me at the crowded train car and wondered what to do. I was relatively new to this whole nursing thing and, thus far, I had always managed to be at home when she needed to nurse. I liked to sit in a special chair with a nursing pillow and a glass of water. It was all very comfortable and familiar. I started feeling a bit panicky thinking of getting her out of the sling and lifting my shirt in front of all these strangers sitting so close to us. It all seemed very complicated. Then I remembered hearing you could nurse in a sling. I fumbled as I reached down, moved the fabric aside, opened my bra, and helped her latch on. She nursed contently and soon drifted off to sleep. I was completely covered by the sling and my seatmates probably never even realized what we were up to. As we were getting off the train several hours later, I got many compliments on my incredibly well-behaved baby. Hmmm…

Babywearing is Good for Caregivers

Babywearing is also good for the caregiver. It frees our hands and lets us get on with our lives. It gives us freedom to go out confidently, knowing that baby has a place where she will be content. Constantly carrying a child makes us physically stronger

One Mother's Perspective:
Reasons I love Babywearing...

Babywearing is not dependent on:

- Where or how you birthed your baby.
- How you feed your baby.
- Where your baby sleeps.
- Whether you are the child's biological parent.
- How you choose to diaper.
- Most medical choices parents make.

For baby, Babywearing:

- Helps at-risk babies learn how to be in the world in a gentle, loving way.
- Helps babies who have had separations from parents recover their bond from that separation.
- Helps adopted babies learn to be comforted by a different rhythm.
- Helps high-need infants learn to integrate the world.
- Helps meet all babies need for early dependence which allows them to be more independent as they get older.

For parents, Babywearing:

- Facilitates attachment parenting for parents who were not parented that way themselves.
- Allows parents to meet a baby's need to be held and their own need to do other tasks.
- Reduces the impact of a high-need baby on daily living for other family members.
- Changes the way parents view a baby's needs.
- Puts parents in closer contact with baby which usually makes it easier to "read" baby.
- Provides a buffer against separations ranging from daily work or separate sleeping to hospitalization.
- Can facilitate breastfeeding and make it easier to breastfeed longer.

Babywearing can begin at birth, in toddlerhood, or even the preschool years. It has benefits at all ages when a child wants or needs to be held. It can extend the ability of a parent to carry a child beyond the "in arms" stage. And it does not rely on politics, religion, or even any specific parenting philosophy to confer its benefits.

Jennifer Rosenberg ("Jenrose")
Founding member of Nine In, Nine Out (NINO)

and allows us to take long walks while including our baby. Wearing our babies can allow us to exercise regularly, walking and even hiking. In our family, we have even made the word "sling" into a verb, as in "Are you going to sling her or am I?" The expectation is that baby will always be in someone's arms.

On a personal note, carriers have made me feel less desperate on those days when my baby wanted to be held all day. We would laugh during those difficult stages and refer to my son as a "Velcro baby" because he needed to be attached to me all day. My husband would encourage me to put a positive spin on the whole experience by saying: "Just think, that is how *important* you are to him!" Well, sure, but I was still worn out sometimes. Being able to put my baby into a soft carrier on those days was always a welcome relief. What was good for baby was definitely good for me! Babywearing gives us happier babies which makes us feel confident and competent.

Babywearing Makes Transitions Easier

A soft carrier feels familiar to baby no matter who is wearing her. Dads, grandparents, and other caregivers can get involved by using a baby carrier. Babies reap the benefits of being held close no matter who is carrying them.

New fathers can sometimes feel left out because of the intense bond between baby and mama, especially if they are a breastfeeding pair. One great way for new dads to bond with their baby is to put baby in a sling and head out the door for a long walk. When our son was born, my husband Erik would take him for walks around the neighborhood in the sling while I had one-on-one time with our older daughter. Our neighbors got to meet our small son, and Dad got some exercise and got to show off the new baby. It is very unlikely that he could have done the same thing with a stroller. Babies who cannot sit up yet tend to get disoriented being pushed along in a stroller and will often get fussy. Having a sling gives you one more option for soothing a cranky baby.

One time we left our small daughter with her grandmother for a few hours. When we returned, both were sound asleep on the bed. I was amazed as my daughter had always nursed to sleep until that day. Later, Grandmom explained that she had just put Nina in the sling and gone about her business. When Nina fell asleep, they both went into the bedroom and took a nap. Genius!

11 year-old Alex wearing our son

On our last family vacation, our small son was carried about happily for hours on the back of an 11 year-old family friend. Our son does not go easily to others, but on her back, he was fine. Such freedom!

Wear Your Baby to Sleep

Babies naturally get lulled to sleep if they are tired and in a soft carrier. Many first time parents marvel that their small baby will nap much longer while in a baby carrier than in a crib or bassinet. Sometimes when baby is too exhausted or overtired to go to sleep, wearing her and walking around the house can provide a wonderful way to soothe her to sleep.

> On those evenings when nothing else works to put our daughter to sleep, my husband dons the [soft carrier] as I walk our sobbing ten week-old daughter from room to room. He settles her in the soft, stretchy fabric and positions her tiny head carefully in the carrier. He pulls the exercise ball up to the desk and bounces vigorously for ten minutes. Her sobs give way to intermittent whimpers. The whimpers diminish to silence; the hardwood floor stops creaking. Eventually, all I can hear is the tip-tapping of the keyboard as my husband rushes to meet his deadline. He is working and simultaneously providing a warm, loving embrace for our sleeping daughter, nestled against his heart.
>
> Sarah, Oregon

Babywearing Can Help Working Mothers Reconnect

One of the most important things that a mother (or a father) who works away from her child can do is *stay connected*. This can be a challenge when mother and baby are separated for many hours each day. One beautiful way to reconnect with your baby after a prolonged separation is to put your baby in a soft carrier and wear your baby while you go about your evening chores. In this way, you can prepare and serve the evening meal, tidy up, return pressing phone calls, do the laundry and such, while simultaneously reconnecting with your baby.

My husband's aunt is a physician. She went back to work full-time when her babies were about six weeks old. Each night when she returned home, she wore her baby close to her heart as she prepared dinner. She says that those are her strongest, happiest memories of being with her sons when they were tiny. Babywearing creates wonderful memories of our little ones.

In a similar manner, you can encourage those who care for your baby in your absence to wear your baby, just as you would if you were there. Babies reap the benefits of being held close, and they feel comforted by the familiarity of the whole sensation. Babywearing can help babies have a *continuity of care* between multiple caregivers.

> I had returned to work, and our nanny was home with my fraternal twin boys. I remember returning one afternoon to find [our nanny] using two blankets to position both babies on her, one in front of her and one on her back. They had each become very cranky due to the beginnings of a cold, and both had wanted to be held. She was able to comfort them in this manner.
>
> Karen, Connecticut

Toddlers Like to be Worn, Too!

While most babywearing occurs when baby is not yet walking, toddlers love the security of the sling. Even after our daughter turned two and was not in the sling on a regular basis, she would ask to be carried in the sling any time she got sick. She enjoyed being worn in the sling at the Aquarium and the Zoo so she could see over the fences and walls.

What about Strollers?

Babywearing and strollers are not mutually exclusive. While I would discourage *overdependenc*e on strollers as our only option for transporting baby, I certainly think there is a time and a place for strollers. Strollers are great for long walks and heavy babies. I personally own and use several different strollers, but strollers are not the first item I reach for when I have a cranky baby. In fact, when I *do* use a stroller, I always slip a soft carrier into the basket to be used when my baby has had enough of riding in the stroller. It almost always gets used…

Strollers are not always as wonderful as we think they will be. Even the fanciest strollers with the most attached baby toys can only contain baby for so long. We have all seen a mother juggling a heavy baby on her hip while trying to maneuver an empty stroller through the mall with one hand. "That mama needs a sling!" we always sympathize. Babies usually are content much longer carried than in a stroller. Baby carriers are much more compact and easier to bring along, and they are wonderful for places that are notoriously unfriendly to strollers (crowded stores with no space to maneuver a stroller, buildings with many steps and no elevators, hiking trails, or anyplace without paved surfaces to push the stroller). While you can wear your baby while you do chores, you cannot really use a stroller inside your home.

For traveling, babywearing cannot be beat. At airports these days, you have to fold your stroller and send it through the conveyor belt. Soft carriers are much less bulky to manage. Public transportation is also much easier with a soft carrier than with a stroller.

> We live in New York City and have to do a lot of walking and traveling by subway. A stroller is just too bulky to lug up and down subway stairs everyday. In her soft carrier, Chloe felt very secure. I felt safe taking her on public transportation and didn't have to worry that she could fall if the train or bus turned or stopped suddenly. For the first year, we went almost everywhere with baby strapped on.
>
> Rebecca, New York

Many newborns get disoriented lying flat on their back in a stroller. As baby gets older and is able to sit up and look around, you may find a stroller to be an attractive option provided that baby is content in it. If we are careful to respect a baby's wishes and hold our babies when they signal the need, strollers can be a welcome addition to our lifestyle. We can make babywearing the norm and use strollers sparingly and appropriately.

Babywearing and Attachment Parenting

Babywearing can be an important component of attachment parenting which may also include breastfeeding and sleeping near baby. Attached parents honor the bonds between parents and children and pay careful attention to the emotional needs of their children in addition to their physical needs. Attached parents acknowledge that babies have a fundamental need to spend large quantities of time near their parents, and this need is joyfully and attentively met. In fact, one main theme of attachment parenting is keeping baby close day and night so that baby develops in a strong, healthy, happy manner. Attachment parenting means responding to baby and meeting baby's needs. Attachment parenting fosters independence in babies by meeting their needs with the understanding that a need that is satisfied goes away.

> Attachment Parenting is the philosophy and practice of parenting methods that foster strong, healthy emotional bonds between parents and children. This approach values responsiveness to the infant or child's physical and emotional needs, nurturing their trust that those needs will be met. Although supported by current research, Attachment Parenting is rooted in the oldest human traditions of all cultures and is anything but new.
>
> Attachment Parenting International

I believe strongly in the principles of attachment parenting, and I have watched with delight as my two children, my now four-year-old daughter and 23-month-old son, have grown strong and confident. I believe in handling children. I believe in filling a child's emotional cup at home so he can later go forth and face the world. But no matter what the parenting philosophy, investing in a good baby carrier is always a wise choice. ***Happy babies make for happier parents, and baby carriers make babies happy.***

Happy baby, happy mama!

Occasionally, I get that fierce feeling that all parents get: *I would do anything for my children,* I think. *I would give them a kidney if they needed it. I would step in front of a moving car. I would chop off my arm.* The truth is most children do not require such a dramatic one-time sacrifice, but what they do need is our constant, ever-loving care. Sometimes, when I am at my wits end with a crying baby or a demanding toddler and I react less than lovingly, I am struck by the irony: here I am willing to give up a kidney, but I begrudge my child a little patience or a brief moment of comfort. It is such a small sacrifice, but picking up a whining child for the fifth time while trying to clean the kitchen can sometimes seem harder than giving up a kidney. I have to remind myself that all our babies want is a bit of kindness and warmth. Let's give our babies what they actually need: lots of in-arms time, love and gentleness at night, breastfeeding on cue (when possible), and not just the empty promise to cut off our arm or donate a kidney.

Parenting Role Models for the Next Generation

One of the most rewarding aspects of wearing my babies has been watching my daughter mimic the way I mother her younger sibling. She and her friends lift their shirts to "nurse" their dolls, and they walk around with their dolls attached to their bodies with whatever long piece of fabric they can find. They are learning how to mother by watching the mothers around them. We have such a powerful influence on our children's lives this way. We can plant the seeds now, and later on if they choose to be parents, they will perhaps treat their children in the gentle affirming way we have modeled for them.

What we do now as parents has a tremendous effect on the way our children will choose to parent later on. I remember in medical school when we were studying the factors that contribute to successful breastfeeding, one of the major factors that predicted breastfeeding success was whether the woman had herself been breastfed as an infant. The next most important factor was if she had a close female role model (sister, aunt, friend, neighbor) whom she had witnessed breastfeeding. We can influence the way the next generation of babies is cared for by simply caring for our own babies in a responsive, gentle manner. *I am convinced that it is in our power to create a* **culture** *for our children where breastfeeding and wearing our babies is the norm.*

While our parenting style may seem unfamiliar to the children and adults around us, we can gently introduce babywearing as an idea. The more children and adults are exposed to it, the less threatening and strange it will seem. Funny misunderstandings, like the one below, will become a rarity.

> I have a sling that is very pretty. I had my three-month-old in it. When my five-year-old niece saw it for the first time, she laughed and said: "What is he doing in your purse?"
>
> Stacey, Tennessee

A beautiful way to contribute to the baby friendly culture is to select toys, books, and playthings for our children that reflect our parenting values. (Please see the Appendix for a list of children's books that include babywearing.) Many baby carrier companies offer child-sized slings so older children can carry their own "babies" (www.taylormadeslings.com, www.rebozoway.org, www.newnativebaby.com and www.mayawrap.com). A great gift idea for a new big brother or sister is a sling that matches mommy and daddy's sling so they can participate by wearing their doll on walks while mom or dad carries the new baby. There is no need to buy anything; however, a shawl or large scarf will work just fine if tied properly. My daughter actually just uses my carriers and folds and rolls them until they fit her.

Child-sized sling

When your child engages in imaginative play – role modeling with dolls or figurines – supply her with mother dolls who 'choose' to breastfeed and father dolls with tiny slings or backpacks. Toss the baby bottles that come with most dolls or call them 'sippy cups with water' as we do in our house. You can make your own doll slings with small handkerchiefs or swatches of fabric or enjoy some of the pre-made ones. My daughter has a set of plastic dollhouse dolls and one of her favorite games is to play "attach the baby." We tie the baby to each caregiver – mama, daddy, auntie, grandma, grandpa in turn – using cloth diaper wipes. If you prefer, Magic Cabin

Babywearing dolls

Dolls (www.magiccabin.com) offers beautiful wooden dollhouse dolls with soft baby carriers in a variety of multicultural family sets.

We are not only role-modeling for our children, but the adults in our lives are learning from our parenting choices as well. Many babywearing mothers report that their husbands, parents, brothers, and sisters like what they see and are anxious to try babywearing for themselves. They see that baby is calm and contented while in the carrier and want that opportunity to bond as well. What we put forth as "normal" baby care can become the standard for many caregivers in our child's life.

> At the Detroit Auto show, I was getting tired from carrying my large nine-month-old through the crowds in my sling. My husband carried him in the sling the rest of the day in front of all those car guys. He did not give it a second thought. Babywearing 'wears off' on the other people in your family without any effort on your part.
>
> Charlotte, Oklahoma

Why does Babywearing Work?

> It is only once babies are born that they learn (or need) to cry. By wearing our precious babies, we create an environment for them that is as close to the perfection of the womb as we can make it.
>
> Jennifer Norton
> Creator of *TheBabyWearer.com*
> On-line Babywearing Resource Center

All babies are born "pre mature" in the sense that they cannot walk, talk, or meet their own needs. It is the price of being upright. Experts theorize that the evolution of human beings walking upright caused the narrowing of the pelvic outlet, necessitating human babies with smaller heads and, thus, smaller brains. In fact, human babies more closely resemble a fetus neurologically than a fully mature infant mammal. Nature has done a brilliant job of maximizing the size of the brain while minimizing the size of the head. Babies' skulls are not fully fused, leaving fontanels (soft spots) which allow the skull to compress during delivery. Hormones during birth allow the ligaments of the mother's pelvis to stretch even more. Even with these adaptations, as any woman who has given birth in the past century can attest, it is still a rather tight fit. Ultimately, we cannot keep our babies inside long enough to fully mature the brain without the head getting too big for delivery. Babywearing allows for the continuation of a womb-like environment, giving the baby a chance for optimal brain and nervous system development.

Imagine a small baby tucked peacefully in a baby carrier. Let us share her world. Small babies do not have a very developed temperature regulation system. They do not retain heat well and get chilled easily. Being held close to another person allows a baby to share the warmth. A baby recognizes familiar smells and enjoys the warmth while being carried. She may smell the milk nearby and thus be inspired to nurse more regularly. The movement feels very similar to the movement she experienced *in utero* and is soothing. Constant movement helps a baby's digestive system. She may spit up less and it may even help with reflux, a common newborn condition. A newborn has several reflexes that persist outside the womb, reflexes that make her startle easily. Swaddling works well to calm these overactive reflexes, and a baby is essentially swaddled while held closely in a sling. Baby's head and spine are properly supported when cradled in a sling. Even when she falls asleep, she can safely be left in the carrier.

As baby grows, the sling provides a "safety zone" of sorts - place where baby can experience the world: the sights, the sounds, the smells, the jostling, the movements of life - while still in the loving embrace of mama.

No one can express the delights of a sling better than a recent sling baby herself. When my daughter was two, she would often speak for her then newborn brother. She would tell me:

> *Mommy, do you know why the baby is crying? He wants to be in the sling. Do you know why the baby wants to be in the sling? He wants to be warm and cozy. He feels good in there. He's nice and happy.*

Well said.

References

[1] Hunziker UA, Barr RG. 1986. "Increased carrying reduces infant crying: A randomized controlled trial." *Pediatrics* 77:641-648.

[2] Barr RG, McMullan SJ, Spiess H, et al. 1991. "Carrying as colic 'therapy': a randomized controlled trial." *Pediatrics* 87:623-630.

[3] Powell A., "Children need touching and attention, Harvard researchers say." *Harvard Gazette* April 9, 1998.

[4] Van Ijsendoorn MH, Hubbard FO. 2000. "Are infant crying and maternal responsiveness during the first year related to infant mother attachment at 15 months?" *Attach Hum Dev* 2(3):371-91.

[5] Waltraud S, Nitsch P, Wassmer G, Roth B. 2002. "Cardiorespiratory stability of premature and term infants carried in infant slings." *Pediatrics* 110:879-883.

[6] Chwo MJ, Anderson GC, Good M, Dowling DA, Shiau SH, Chu DM. 2002. "A randomized controlled trial of early kangaroo care for preterm infants: effects on temperature, weight, behavior and and acuity. *J Nurs Res* 10(2):129-42.

[7] Conde-Agudelo A, Diaz-Rossello JL, Balizan JM. 2003. "Kangaroo mother care to reduce morbidity and mortality in low birthweight infants. *Cochrane Database Syst Rev* (2): CD002771.

[8] Schanberg S, Field T. 1987. "Sensory deprivation stress and supplemental stimulation in the rat pup and preterm human neonate." *Child Development* 58:1431-1447.

[9] James-Roberts I St, Hurry J, Bowyer J, Barr RG. 1995. "Supplementary carrying compared with advice to increase responsive parenting as interventions to prevent persistent infant crying." *Pediatrics* 95:381-388.

[10] Adamson-Macedo EN. 1990. "The effects of touch on preterm and fullterm neonates and young children." *J Reprod Infant Psychol* 8:267-273.

[11] Sponseller D. 1994. "Bone, Joint and Muscle Problems: Developmental Dysplaisa of the Hip" pp. 1018- 1020. in *Principles and Practice of Pediatrics, Second Edition.* Frank Oski et al, ed. Philadelphia: J.B. Lippincott Company.

[12] Aronsson DD, et al. 1994. "Developmental dysplasia of the hip." *Pediatrics.* 94(2 Pt 1):201-8.

[13] Roper A. 1976. "Hip dysplasia in the African Bantu." *J Bone Joint Surg Br.* 58(2):155-8.

[14] Ang KC, et al. 1997. "An epidemiological study of developmental dysplasia of the hip in infants in Singapore." *Ann Acad Med Singapore.* 26(4):456-8.

[15] Sears W, Sears M. 1993 *The Baby Book: Everything You Need to Know About Your Baby from Birth to Age Two.* Boston: Little, Brown and Company. pp. 262-292.

[16] Anisfeld E, Casper V, Nozyce M, Cunningham N. 1990. "Does infant carrying promote attachment? An experimental study of the effects of increased physical contact on the development of attachment." *Child Dev* 61:1617-1627.

[17] Tessier R, Cristo M, Velez S, Giron M, Ruiz-Palaez JG, Charpak Y, Charpak N. 1998. "Kangaroo mother care and the bonding hypothesis." *Pediatrics* 102:e17.

[18] Dihigo SK. 1998. "New strategies for the treatment of colic: modifying the parent/infant interaction." *J Pediatr Health Care* 12(5):256-62.

[19] Bowlby, J. 1983 *Attachment.* 2nd edition. New York: Basic Books. pp. 356-357.

[20] Blurton Jones, N, ed. 1972. *Ethnological Studies of Child Behavior.* Cambridge: Cambridge University Press.

[21] Allport, S. 1997. *A Natural History of Parenting: From Emperor Penguins to Reluctant Ewes, a Naturalist Looks at How Parenting Differs in the Animal World and Ours.* New York: Harmony Books, pp. 158-159.

Chapter 2

Babywearing in Special Situations

Wearing Multiples

When faced with having more than one baby at a time, it can be a challenge to find enough hands for everyone. Babywearing can facilitate life with multiples. Babywearing gives you one more tool to use as you juggle the needs of your babies and the rest of your family. Although wearing more than one baby at a time can certainly be done, especially in the early months when the babies are tiny, more often mothers of multiples report that they use their sling to hold one baby while the other is otherwise occupied. If you do choose to wear two babies at a time, you have several options. Some mothers like to crisscross two slings and wear a baby on each hip. It can be wonderful to watch the two interact as they sit face-to-face on either hip. In the same manner, you may wear a baby in front and a baby in back in two crisscrossed slings. Most mothers prefer unpadded slings or even simple tube pouches if they are wearing two slings in order to minimize bulk. If you prefer, you may use a specially made front pack for your multiples such as the Weego Twin (www.weego.com).

The most routine outings can become a logistical puzzle when you have multiple babies to tote.

Twin front pack
Used with permission

With newborn twins and a three year old, I find lots of ways to use my slings. In their early days, I used a sling around the house to keep at least one of the babies out of my active toddler's reach. Now that they are a little older (3 months old), I have begun to venture out of the house with all three girls in tow. I find what works best is to have one baby in a sling, carry the other one in her car seat carrier, and hold my three-year-old's hand. We can even go shopping this way with the toddler facing me in the shopping cart, one baby in her car seat carrier in the large part of the cart, and one baby on me in the sling. This doesn't leave much room for groceries, but it works when I just need a few things. I have not found it very practical to carry both babies in slings simultaneously. For one thing, it is very heavy! I also find that I don't end up with either hand free, as I need them to help support the babies.

Theresa, Texas

Wearing your babies can provide the support necessary to nurse both babies simultaneously.

I crisscrossed the two slings in the back so that I had one baby on each side. I wore overalls with tank tops and button down shirts. I would release whichever side I needed to nurse on, and pull up the tank. It was easy, modest, and most of all comforting for my kids.

Martha, Ohio

However you choose to incorporate babywearing into your daily routine with your multiples, know that you are giving each baby exactly what she needs: plenty of interaction, physical contact, and nurturing.

Adoptive Babywearing Promotes Bonding

Babywearing is good for all babies, but it may be especially important for the baby who joins the family through adoption. Babies who join the family through adoption may experience a sort of attachment disruption when they leave their previous caregivers. Recent studies have demonstrated the vital importance of maternal responsiveness and mother-baby attachment to the social and cognitive development of the adopted child.[1,2] Wearing this baby helps her feel warm and safe and connected to her new family.

Babies who have been in multiple care situations before being adopted are especially vulnerable to attachment disorders later on and stand to benefit greatly from lots of physical contact and holding in their new family. Many adoptive families report that wearing their baby helps them feel closer to their newly acquired baby, and they can visibly see their baby relax when they are close to mom or dad.

Wear your adopted baby!

We adopted our daughter when she was a week old. I had used a sling with our (biological) son for many years, and we both loved it. I would strongly urge all adoptive mothers to consider using a sling and breastfeeding their babies. My favorite memories are of having her in the sling and walking around the house, looking down at her and smiling together. Slings are also wonderful as they discourage other people from holding babies who often need to be connecting with their new mama, not other friends and relatives.

Molly, Washington

Families adopting older babies may find that new parenting is a very different experience for them than for those adopting newborns or younger babies. Suddenly acquiring a full-grown, walking, talking toddler can be quite a shock.

Our daughter, born in Guatemala, arrived home at 16 months old, a full toddler. The staff at [agency] stressed that our daughter's entire world would be changing for her, and for us to try and keep everything the same for her, no matter how small.

These are the thing that I feel are most important when adopting an older baby:
- Recreate infancy by holding your child for the first full year after arrival home.
- Don't confuse the child by doing "pass the baby" – the child needs time to learn about his new parents.
- Listen to your child, not well-meaning advice from other adults. Your child knows what she needs and how much closeness she requires.

- Read as much as you can before the child arrives and talk to adoption professionals and other adoptive parents.
- Get as much data as possible from the child's caregivers so that you can recreate familiar things in the child's new world.

Susan, New Jersey

Some of the benefits of wearing the adoptive baby are purely practical. Parents who adopt an older baby often report muscle soreness from suddenly needing to constantly lift and carry a heavy child. They have not had a chance to gradually get accustomed to the weight. Carriers may alleviate some of this discomfort.

> The benefits of babywearing for me were that I was able to carry Alexa (adopted at 14 months old) and hold her close to me for much longer than I would have been able to without a carrier. Many of the other adopting parents complained about sore arms and thumbs from lifting and carrying the children. I never had a problem with this because of the carrier.

Madalyn, Texas

Adoption is simply the way a child joins a family. By responding to your baby's needs, you will become the expert on the newest member of your family.

Wearing the Special Needs Baby

Babywearing can be a therapeutic tool for special needs babies. Special needs children clearly benefit from being touched and held, and wearing our special needs babies gives us a way to touch and hold them while meeting our own need to get things done.

Several studies have demonstrated the benefits of touch for special needs children. A 2002 study looked at a group of children who had a range of disabilities (including cerebral palsy, asthma, sensory impairments, and Down's syndrome) and found that after teaching parents simple massage techniques, parents reported improvements in their children's muscle tone, joint mobility, sleep patterns, and bowel movements. Parents also reported that they themselves had benefited by feeling "closer" to their child and less stressed.[3]

Wearing Foster Babies
One Foster Family's Story

Reedy Hickey and her husband P.J. have fostered over 30 children using Attachment Parenting principles. This is their story.

We take care of our foster babies as if they were our own birth children in every way, except that they are bottle-fed. We hold them as much as we can. I wear them in a sling all of the time when I am out in public, and we never take the car seat out of the car. We sleep in close proximity to them; we have a porta-crib next to our bed. We feed them bottles, but use a breastfeeding model: holding them close, never propping the bottle, changing sides for eye/hand coordination, feeding on demand yet being careful not to overfeed them formula which is not a concern with breastmilk. ***We answer their needs as quickly as is humanly possible, helping them to feel as if they are the most precious beings on this earth.***

Of our 31 fostered babies, five have returned to their birth parents and the remainder have been adopted. One of the ways we encourage the adoptive parents who receive our foster babies to try attachment parenting is by giving each of them a sling and a copy of The Baby Book by Dr. William Sears and Martha Sears. We also let them know how we have parented their baby for the first weeks or months of his or her life which includes wearing them in a sling. We place importance on the fact that adopted babies need this closeness to attach to their new parents. It appears to be working. We are deeply gratified to know that a number of [the adoptive families] have used or are using attachment-style parenting techniques.

Teaching a child how to trust is one of the greatest gifts we can give a child.

Excerpted with permission from Hickey, Reedy and PJ. "Interview with Reedy and PJ Hickey" Attachment Parenting: The Journal of Attachment Parenting International. 7(2):1 and 9, 2004.

Several studies have reported on the importance of touch for children diagnosed with autism. In a study published in 2002, parents of autistic children were surveyed after attending a touch therapy program. Parents reported that routine tasks were accomplished more easily, and their children appeared generally more relaxed. Parents felt that the touch therapy opened a communication channel between themselves and their children.[4] In a study published a year earlier, researchers found improvements in the behavior of autistic children following massage therapy. Their results suggested that the children in the massage group showed more on-task and social relatedness behavior during play and experienced fewer sleep problems at home.[5] In another study of autistic children, those who were treated with modified holding therapy showed significantly more positive behavior changes.[6]

One type of special needs baby who can benefit from being worn is an infant who has been diagnosed with "failure to thrive." This condition is defined as infants who are slow to gain weight for a variety of medical and/or social reasons. We know that babies who are held close are inspired to nurse more. Also, the movement associated with babywearing soothes babies and helps them to cry less. The energy they would have spent crying and fussing can now be put to better use to help them gain weight and thrive.

> We adopted our child when he was eight months old. He had been in four other homes and had attachment issues. He was drug affected and had been diagnosed with failure to thrive. He had been abused and neglected and was often kept in a car seat for prolonged periods of time. I put him in my sling right away, and he loved it. His head changed shape from being flattened right away. At two, he is attached and well-adjusted and still asks for me to carry him in his 'baby.'
>
> Alissa, Iowa

Babies who are physically challenged can especially benefit from being worn. Babies who suffer from cerebral palsy or other forms of neurological birth defects often have increased muscle tone resulting in muscle rigidity and spasms. By holding them close to our body in a soft carrier, we encourage their muscles to mold to the contours of our body, increasing flexibility. We provide gentle, constant vestibular stimulation (the vestibulus is the fluid filled organ in the ear that helps regulate balance) simply by moving around. Baby constantly readjusts in harmony with our movements. Babywearing also promotes healthy muscle development.

Children with developmental delays continue to reap great benefits through the upright positioning, symmetrical positioning, vestibular stimulation, and the positioning of the lower extremities in abduction that carrying in a physiologically advantageous position offers. When baby rides in a carrier where the legs dangle down (a more adducted position), this effect is not achieved. When they are older, being carried gives them a chance to experience a broader range of events and emotions than being positioned in a chair, for example.

Lilian Holm-Drumgole
Physical Therapist, Developer of the Baby Back-Tie Carrier

As parents, we are often ready to spend huge sums of money to provide our special needs children with the best infant stimulation gadgets and techniques when, in fact, the best (and least expensive!) method is to simply wear our baby as often as we can.

Sometimes the benefits of wearing your special needs baby show up much later in childhood.

My five-year-old had been having many meltdowns. We were starting to get concerned so we began a long process of trying to find the cause. Eventually, he was found to have issues with sensory integration [*a term that describes children who are especially sensitive to external sensory stimuli*]. Our occupational therapist asked if he had been carried as a baby. I said, yes, that he had lived in his sling for the first six months of his life and whenever he wanted after that. Her response made me happy. She told me that had he NOT been carried all that time, his issues would probably be three times worse than they are.

Julie, Florida

Special needs babies thrive on many of the same things that make other babies happy. Carry your baby with confidence and encourage all his caregivers to do the same.

Wearing the Critically Ill Baby

When a previously healthy baby suddenly becomes gravely ill, parents are forced into a role they may never have expected. It is a terrible thing to watch a baby suffer, and parents of acutely ill children often scramble to find ways to comfort their distressed little ones. Watching a child in pain can bring out feelings of helplessness and rage in parents. Parents often report that they wish there was something they could do ease their child's suffering. Maintaining closeness and being a constant presence for a critically ill baby is one way to positively participate in her care. Here

When Parents Have Special Needs

Babywearing can provide extra support for parents who have special needs. Parents who have limited vision or hearing may use babywearing as a way of keeping baby close. This proximity helps a parent respond promptly to baby's body signals and movements rather than relying on the sound cues (crying, fussing, etc.) or the visual cues (rooting, grimacing) that hearing and seeing parents might use. Wearing baby in a soft carrier can also free up both hands allowing a deaf parent to sign.

I am deaf, and I use sign language to communicate. I have a 4-month-old baby and an 18-month-old toddler. At times, one of them wants to be carried and the other needs my attention. I can't do both at the same time, so it works for me to carry the baby in my sling, then pick up the toddler if she needs my attention. I can walk and sign with my toddler while carrying my baby in the sling. I feel better knowing that I am paying attention to both of them. I feel comfortable carrying one of them inside my sling because I can feel her if she cries, fusses, or giggles. I always depend on feeling her and her voice to know what she is doing and it helps us to make a strong bond. In public, I always keep the baby in my carrier and watch the toddler in the shopping cart. If I didn't use a sling, who knows what would happen to them, and it scares me to think that if something happened, I couldn't hear them. Using a sling makes it a lot easier for me to sign with my husband when we go out shopping. I love my sling. I encourage others to use it because it is impossible to hold the baby and sign at the same time. When I first saw a sling, I thought that it would be easier for me to sign so I tried it and I loved it.

Melissa, Minnesota

Annalysa wearing Sage
(Used with permission)

Parents with limited mobility (for example: parents in wheelchairs or parents who have arthritis) can use soft baby carriers to their advantage.

My greatest ally in managing a newborn on my own was the baby sling. Being in a chair and trying to carry a baby at the same time felt not unlike having both arms and both legs tied behind my back. The baby sling, and later a front pack freed my arms and let me accomplish things while holding Sage.[7]

Annalysa, Montana

is a story of how babywearing proved to be an invaluable tool as a way of comforting this critically ill little boy.

On December 30, our son Elijah joined us. He was in his new sling within a few hours of birth. The next three days were blissful! We took turns wearing him skin-to-skin in the sling and he was very content.

On the third day after birth, he was unexpectedly diagnosed with congenital heart defects. Although everything looked normal, his pediatrician decided to investigate his slightly dusky gums during a routine newborn exam. Within a few hours, our world was suddenly turned upside down. We were told that our precious son would need to have emergency open-heart surgery in order to survive.

We almost lost him during surgery that night. The next few days were rocky and difficult. We stayed with him as much as possible. Elijah did amazingly well and had his second surgery at ten days of age. Originally we were told to expect a stay of about a month total. However, his care team noticed that the times when he was with his mommy (almost always skin-to-skin), his vital signs were stable and they decided to let him go home early. He was discharged after 13 days in the ICU and only five days after his second surgery!

The next few weeks were hard. We brought home a scared, defensive newborn who was easily startled, didn't want to be touched for fear of being hurt, and was in pain. He cried all the time and would wake up from a deep sleep screaming! We had been warned to expect this from the PICU care team. They said his trust had been violated - albeit to save his life - and we just needed to be patient while he healed. Thank goodness for the sling! The sling was our savior! As soon as we put him in the sling, he would stop crying or at least could be soothed. Since he was born in winter, we were warned not to let him get cold as it would stress his heart. I spent a lot of time skin-to-skin with him in a fleece pouch with a robe on all day!

Within a few months, the transformation was amazing! This fussy, defensive little one became the most laid back, happy baby we have ever been around! Today at 18 months, he still spends a lot of time in the sling and is a living, breathing example of the benefits of babywearing!

Julie, Illinois

Sometimes, babywearing can soothe both mother and child when illness forces unexpected compromises in their lives.

Timmy was born on June 25th, and my life was perfect. Three weeks postpartum, I got the worst phone call of my life. They called me to tell me I had Hepatitis C [a virus that attacks the liver and is considered incurable and life-threatening]. I realized I had contracted the virus when I had open-heart surgery as a child. To my horror, Timmy came back positive for Hepatitis C as well. I got the news that [my disease was advanced] and I needed to start treatment to try and clear the virus or I would need a liver transplant. [Treatment is incompatible with breastfeeding.] I chose to delay my own treatment and to continue to breastfeed Timmy to ten months to help his immune system. Knowing I was going to have to give up breastfeeding was excruciating for me. And all the fears of losing my baby and myself to this disease were a constant daily battle. That's when we turned to the sling. I needed to feel close to him. Sometimes I just squeezed him and inhaled the sweet smell of his beautiful face. During those horrible weeks of weaning, the sling was our only comfort as I walked him around crying with him over our loss.

I am now on treatment that is similar to chemo and leaves me tired, and I don't know what the outcome will be and that is terrifying. I am grateful for these sweet days in our sling, feeling him breathing against my chest and being one, even if just for awhile.

Jennifer, New Jersey

Critically ill babies are not the only hospitalized babies who stand to benefit from babywearing. In the next chapter, we will see that premature babies thrive on being worn, too.

References

[1] Stams GJ, Juffer F, van IJsendoorn MH. 2002. "Maternal sensitivity, infant attachment, and temperament in early childhood predict adjustment in middle childhood: the case of adopted children and their biologically unrelated parents." *Dev Psychol.* Sep. 38(5):806-21.

[2] Juffer F, Hoksbergen RA, Riksen-Walraven JM, Kohnstamm GA. 1997. "Early intervention in adoptive families: supporting maternal sensitive responsiveness, infant-mother attachment, and infant competence.*" J Child Psychol Psychiatry.* Nov. 38(8):1039-50.

[3] Cullen L, Barlow J. 2002. "Kiss, cuddle, squeeze: the experiences and meaning of touch among parents of children with autism attending a Touch Therapy Programme." *J Child Health Care,* Sep 6(3):171-81.

[4] Barlow J, Cullen L. 2002. "Increasing touch between parents and children with disabilities: preliminary results from a new programme." *J Fam Health Care.* 12(1):7-9.

[5] Escalona A, Field T, Singer–Strunck R, Cullen C, Hartshorn K. 2001. "Brief report: Improvements in the behavior of children with autism following massage therapy." *J Autism Dev Disord.* Oct. 31(5):513-6.

[6] Rohmann UH, Hartmann H. 1985. [Modified holding therapy. A basic therapy in the treatment of autistic children] *Z Kinder Jugendpsychiatr.* 13(3):182-98.

[7] Excerpted with permission from Lovos, Annalysa. 2004. "On the Day Sage Was Born" Mothering: The Magazine of Natural Living. 126:53-55.

Used with permission

Chapter 3

Kangaroo Care of the Premature Infant

Nowhere are newborn babies more closely studied than in the neonatal intensive care unit. Premature infants attract the attention of medical professionals who carefully monitor daily intake, temperature, oxygen saturation, weight, nutrition, growth, and development. The neonatal intensive care unit is one place where the medical community has been intensely interested in the benefits of skin-to-skin contact because the consequences are so immediate and profound for their patients. By turning our attention to the use of babywearing techniques to care for premature infants, we get a rare glimpse into the world of the highly medicalized, life and death benefits of skin-to-skin contact.

Prematurity is a real issue in the United States today. A premature infant is defined as an infant born at an estimated gestational age of less than 37 weeks. As dating may not always be accurate, a more precise method of determining prematurity uses birth weight to describe newborns. Low birth weight (LBW) describes infants with a birth weight below 2500 grams. Very low birth weight (VLBW) describes infants with a birth weight of 1001-1500 grams. Recent estimates show that low birth weight occurs in about seven per 100 live births in the United States. In fact, we all probably either know someone who has had a baby prematurely, or we have ourselves had a baby prematurely. It is an issue that affects all of us.

How can we help premature babies survive and thrive? In the past, we have acted aggressively to save these small babies. With incubators and invasive medicine, we have pushed the boundaries of what was considered a viable baby. Fifty years ago, a baby born at 32 weeks was considered very premature and had a poor prognosis. Today, babies born as early as 23 and 24 weeks are sometimes considered viable. No question, modern medicine has been good to premature babies, but has something been missing?

I would argue that *human touch* has been the vital element missing from our early efforts to care for premature babies. In this chapter, I would like to tell you about an exciting, innovative way of dealing with premature babies called kangaroo care. For those of us who are drawn to attachment style parenting, kangaroo care makes sense instinctively and holds exciting potential for our smallest babies.

KANGAROO MOTHER INTERVENTION (KMI)

The initial motivation for promoting skin-to-skin contact between mother and premature baby was actually largely financial. The original Kangaroo Mother Intervention (KMI) was started in 1978 in Colombia as a way of dealing with overcrowding and minimal resources in hospitals caring for premature babies. KMI is described as an alternative comprehensive care method for LBW infants. The researchers, Rey and Martinez, were the first to value human touch in the care of premature babies, and their work was revolutionary. They had mothers be the incubators instead of the plastic bins. Stable premature babies were monitored during the day at a clinic and then sent home each night with their mother! Intensive care units are very expensive to run, so by sending the babies home each night, the hospitals were able to enjoy significant savings.

This was perhaps motivated by financial concerns, but the results were compelling. Not only were mothers indeed very effective "incubators" for their babies, premature babies who enjoyed skin-to-skin contact with their caregivers *had less severe infections, shorter hospital stays, and breastfed longer.* [1]

The specifics outlined for the original KMI are really quite strict. Parents who are considering KMI for their babies must be prepared to make a significant investment of time and energy to meet the guidelines of KMI. KMI is reserved for medically stable premature babies only. KMI has three main components: kangaroo position, kangaroo nutrition, and kangaroo discharge and follow-up policies.   Low birth weight infants are eligible for both kangaroo position and kangaroo nutrition as soon as they overcome major adaptation problems to extrauterine life (i.e., any infection or concomitant condition has been properly treated), are thriving in a neutral thermal environment, and are able to suck and swallow properly. Let us look at each KMI component more closely:[2]

1. **Kangaroo position:** Baby is clothed only in a diaper and is placed upright and prone directly against mother's bare chest. Baby is often secured with a piece of fabric. This upright position is preferred for premature babies because they often have trouble breathing when they are fully reclined, perhaps due to internal organs pressing upwards on the diaphragm. Skin-to-skin contact is maintained 24 hours a day, even while sleeping. Other caregivers may share the mother's role as a kangaroo position provider. Even while sleeping, kangaroo providers must maintain a semi-sitting position.

Kangaroo Position (upright and prone)

2. **Kangaroo nutrition:** This means exclusive or nearly exclusive breastfeeding based on infant needs rather than on demand. Need-based means that babies might be fed *more* often than they signal in order to achieve appropriate weight gain. Although full-term babies should be fed on cue, preemies may not be neurologically mature enough to signal the need to nurse. Supplements (of pumped breastmilk when available and/or formula) are delivered via dropper to infants with suboptimal weight gains (defined as less than 20 grams per day).

Kangaroo nutrition policies are carefully designed to protect the mother-baby nursing dyad. Mothers are encouraged to pump to maintain their supply if their babies are not able to nurse adequately at the breast. Artificial nipples (bottles, pacifiers) are not used in order to avoid "nipple confusion" - a condition in which a baby gets accustomed to an artificial nipple causing him to suck improperly at the breast - leading to sore nipples for mom and sometimes ultimate rejection of the breast by baby.

3. **Kangaroo discharge and follow-up policies:** Eligible infants are discharged home, regardless of their current weight or gestational age, after successful adaptation to the kangaroo method. (Most hospitals have an arbitrary minimum-weight criteria that a premature baby must reach before being discharged home, even if they are otherwise thriving.) Once at home, infants are kept in the kangaroo position until they do not accept it anymore, usually around 37 weeks of gestational age. After discharge, infants are monitored daily until they recover their birth weight and are gaining at least 20 grams per day. Afterwards, weekly visits are scheduled until term (40 weeks gestational age).

KANGAROO CARE (KC)

Although the original parameters of Kangaroo Mother Intervention have been well-defined, different authors have adopted and adapted diverse components of KMI to suit the particular needs of their little patients. Today the term "kangaroo care" is loosely used to mean any amount of skin-to-skin contact, and it is often even used interchangeably with the term "skin-to-skin contact." Kangaroo Care (KC) is a modified form of the original Kangaroo Mother Intervention. It is much less strict in its guidelines. For example, there is no preset amount of time per day one is expected to keep baby in the kangaroo position. Usually, the other two components of KMI (breastfeeding and early discharge) are not required. *The good news is that even with the littlest bit of skin-to-skin contact, a mere few hours a day in some studies, premature babies still reap the benefits.*

Infant Benefits of Kangaroo Care

Studies of kangaroo care over nearly two decades suggest **improved stability** for infants receiving this intervention.[4,5] Infants receiving KC have improved vital signs, better temperature regulation, and higher mean tympanic temperatures than their counterparts. Temperature regulation in KC infants is at least as good as that obtained

A Closer Look: A Study on Kangaroo Mother Intervention

Researchers and doctors have been anxious to duplicate the positive results of KMI in their own patient populations. One contemporary study followed the strict KMI guidelines and confirmed the success seen in the original work conducted almost 20 years earlier.

Over 1000 infants who were less than 20 grams at birth were followed. Infants were randomly assigned to two groups.

The first group was the kangaroo care group. These infants were kept in an upright position in skin-to-skin contact, firmly attached to the mother's chest for 24 hours a day. Their temperature was maintained within the normal range by the mother's body heat. The infants were breastfed regularly and premature formula supplements were used to guarantee adequate weight gain as necessary. They were examined daily until they gained at least 20 grams per day. They remained in the kangaroo position until they no longer accepted it.

The control intervention infants were kept in incubators until they could regulate their temperature and show appropriate weight gain. They were usually discharged when they weighed 1700 grams. The practice of the neonatal intensive unit was to severely restrict the parent's access to their infants.

Infants who received KMI spent less time in the hospital, the severity of infections was less, and more of these infants were breastfed until three months of corrected age.[g]

---

[g] *Corrected age is postmenstrual age plus post-natal age. Using the corrected age of a premature infant gives us a more realistic picture of what the infant should be like, developmentally, at a given age.*

inside an incubator. Respiratory patterns improve with reduced episodes of apnea (temporary cessation of breathing) and bradycardia (slowing of the heart rate). KC babies have more regular breathing patterns. Transcutaneous oxygen levels do not decrease during KC indicating that oxygen saturation is not compromised.

As discussed previously, KC can **shorten the hospital stay** for a premature baby.[6] Several studies have focused on the **developmental benefits** of KC for infants. We know that babies who receive KC breastfeed better and more often. Additionally, KC accelerates a baby's autonomic nervous system maturation.[7] Babies who receive KC have more rapid maturation of their vagal tone, a major component of our parasympathetic nervous system which helps our system to "rest and digest." This earlier maturation promotes better growth and development. In fact, KC has been found to increase the rate of infant weight gain.[8]

There are **behavioral benefits** of KC for infants. KC improves infant state organization with longer alertness periods, less crying, and more quiet sleep.[9] All the energy that baby would spend on crying, is now able to be spent on growing and developing instead. Much learning is thought to occur during the quiet alert state which describes the periods of time when baby is simply awake and alert, not eating or crying.

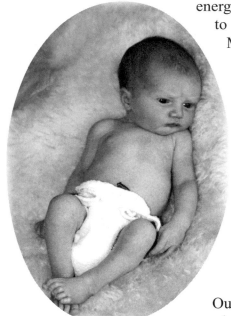

Quiet alert state

One exciting study looked at the **analgesic effect** of KC for infants. KC was found to be a remarkably potent intervention against the pain experienced during heel stick in newborns.[10] Based on this study alone, it is worth our time to ask to hold our babies during immunizations and routine needle sticks.

Our best information about KC comes from large randomized controlled studies of many babies, but we can also learn from studies involving only one baby - specific case studies. Below are several case studies that were interesting and may point the way towards future research. Our first case study involved a baby requiring a mechanical ventilator to breathe. Since most studies of KC are on stabilized preemies, this study provided valuable insight into the use of KC with sick preemies. The researchers found that KC assisted in the baby's recovery from respiratory distress, [11] an interesting finding that indicates future research involving KC should include sick premature infants.

The second case study involved an infant with severe gastroesophageal reflux who benefited from being held in the kangaroo position. [12] Trying kangaroo care for an infant suffering from reflux makes sense. Common treatment of reflux often includes instructions to offer small, frequent feeds and to keep baby upright following feeds. The kangaroo position automatically keeps baby upright. The closeness with mom promotes more frequent nursing sessions, ensuring that baby will not be so hungry from waiting and will take in less at a single feeding.

Another case study described the benefits of triplets kangarooing together.[13]

Maternal Benefits of Kangaroo Care

Babies are not the only ones to benefit from Kangaroo Care, mothers benefit too! KC helps women breastfeed successfully. In one study of very low birth weight infants, kangaroo care was one of the significant correlates that predicted **successful lactation** beyond 40 weeks corrected age.[14] This is, of course, of great benefit to the babies concerned as well. Breastfeeding confers immunological and nutritional benefits to babies which cannot be duplicated with even the fanciest premature formulas. This feature of breastfeeding can be especially essential to a vulnerable preemie.

KC has also been shown to have a positive impact on mother's sense of **competence** and on the **mother-infant attachment** process.[15] Baby is distressed less often and mom feels like she is doing a good job. People tell her she is doing a good job, and she feels validated. It is a loving cycle that reinforces attachment to her baby. Mothers who practice KC are more responsive to their babies. We know now that responsiveness to an infant's cues is perhaps one of the most important building blocks of baby's neurological development. Mother responding to baby allows various neurological pathways to be completed - setting baby up for life! It is a beautiful dance between mother and baby.

***Kangaroo Care promotes
mother-infant attachment.***

Practicing kangaroo care with a pre-term baby allows parents to feel that they are contributing to the care of their baby. This can be very empowering. Parents of preemies are often cast in a passive role: they are expected to sit by and watch machines and other human beings take care of all of their baby's needs. By holding their tiny baby, parents are able to be pro-active, to *do* something concrete to help their child.

Long-term Benefits of Kangaroo Care

Kangaroo Care is clearly beneficial for the premature baby in the early weeks, but the benefits have been shown to extend even further. In one study, infants who received KC were studied at three months corrected age and at six months corrected age. At three months, mothers and fathers were more sensitive and provided a better home environment. At six months, KC mothers were more sensitive and infants had higher mental and psychomotor development. Thus, KC has both a *direct* impact on infant development by contributing to neurophysiological organization and an *indirect* effect by improving parental mood, perceptions, and interactive behavior.[16]

We can change the world for the better if we improve the way we care for premature babies. So wear your baby, premature or not!

References

[1] Rey E, Martinez H. 1983. "Manejo Racional del Nino Prematuro." Bogota, Colombia: Universidad Nacional.

[2] Charpak N, Ruiz-Palaez JG, Figueroa de Calume Z. 1996. "Current knowledge of Kangaroo Mother Intervention." *Curr Opin Pediatr.* 8(2):108-12.

[3] Charpak N, Ruiz-Palaez JG, Figueroa de Calume Z, Charpak Y. 2001. "A randomized, controlled trial of Kangaroo Mother Care: Results of follow-up at one year of corrected age." *Pediatrics.* 108(5):1072-9.

[4] Bohnhorst G, et al. 2001. "Skin-to-skin (kangaroo care), respiratory control, and thermoregulation." *Journal of Pediatrics.* 138 (2):193-197.

[5] Anderson GC. 1991. "Current knowledge about skin-to-skin (kangaroo) care for preterm infants." *J Perinatol.* 11:216-226.

[6] Charpak N, Ruiz-Palaez JG, Figueroa de Calume Z, Charpak Y. 2001. "A randomized, controlled trial of Kangaroo Mother Care: Results of follow-up at one year of corrected age." *Pediatrics.* 108(5):1072-9.

[7] Feldman R, Eidelman AI. 2003. "Skin-to skin contact (Kangaroo Care) accelerates autonomic and neurobeharioural maturation in preterm infants." *Dev Med Child Neurol.* 45(4): 274-81.

[8] Conde-Agudelo A, Diaz-Rossello JL, Balizan JM. 2003. "Kangaroo mother care to reduce morbidity and mortality in low birthweight infants." *Cochrane Database Syst Rev.* (2): CD002771.

[9] Ibid.

[10] Gray L, Watt L., Blass E. 2000. "Skin-to-skin contact is analgesic in healthy newborns." *Pediatrics.* 105(1):e14. (www.pediatrics.org/cgi/content/full/105/1/e14)

[11] Swinth JY, Anderson GC, Hadeed AJ. 2003. "Kangaroo (skin-to-skin) Care with a preterm infant before, during and after mechanical ventilation." *Neonatal Netw.* 22(6): 33-8.

[12] Roller CG. 1999. "Kangaroo care for a restless infant with gastric reflux: One nurse midwife's personal experience." *MCN: The American Journal of Maternal-Child Nursing* 24(5): 244-245.

[13] Swinth JY, et al. 2000. "Shared kangaroo care for triplets." *MCN: The American Journal of Maternal-Child Nursing.* 25(4): 214-215.

[14] Furman L, Minich N, Hack M. 2002. "Correlates of lactation in mothers of very low birth weight infants." *Pediatrics.* 109(4): e57. (www.pediatrics.org/cgi/content/full/109/4/e57)

[15] Tessier R, Cristo M, Velez S, Giron M, Ruiz-Palaez JG, Charpak Y, Charpak N. 1998. "Kangaroo mother care and the bonding hypothesis." *Pediatrics.* 102:e17.

[16] Feldman, R. Eidelmen A, Sirota L, Weller A. 2002. "Comparison of skin-to-skin (kangaroo) and traditional care: Parenting outcomes and preterm infant development." *Pediatrics.* 110(1):16-26.

Babywearing is for everyone

Fathers

Mothers

Grandmothers

Little Boys

Little Girls

Growing up in a sling

2 weeks old
Padded ring sling
Cradle Hold

2 months old
Pouch
Back - Reclined

4 months old
Pouch ring sling
Kangaroo Carry

13 months old
Hip Sling
Hip Carry

20 months old
Unpadded Ring Sling
Back Carry

The Many Ways to Carry Baby on Your Back

Pouch

Fabric Pack (newborn)

Fabric Pack (toddler)

Wraparound

Tie-sling

Constructed Pack

Wraparound

Contemporary Babywearing

Washing dishes

Sweeping

Ways babywearing can make your life easier

Used with permission

At the beach

Breastfeeding discreetly

Hands free for older child

Sleeping through a picnic on mama's back

Part II:

Choosing and Using Your Baby Carrier

In Part I, we covered the "why" of babywearing: the many benefits of this tradition. In Part II, we will turn to the "how" of babywearing. Consider this your own personal babywearing how-to guide.

We will start with basic babywearing tips and safety. Subsequent chapters will help you choose the carrier that is right for you and your baby and help you use it to your satisfaction.

Babywearing is a learned skill. The best way to get proficient at wearing your baby is to practice wearing your baby often. Let's get started…

Chapter 4

Babywearing Basics

When I became a new mom, I did my research and was convinced that I wanted to wear my baby. I was a little unclear on the specifics, however. Exactly how many hours a day was I supposed to wear my baby? Could I put her down when she was sleeping or was I supposed to continue carrying her? How about when I needed to sit at my desk and pay bills?

Four years later, I now have experience wearing my daughter as well as her younger brother. Let me share what our experience has been like. When my daughter was a newborn, I carried her almost constantly in a sling. Practically speaking, most babies in a carrier like for the caregiver to be *moving* at least until baby falls asleep. I discovered that when I first put her in the sling awake, it was best to leave her head out of the sling and get busy doing activities that required movement, such as laundry or yard work. She would then fall asleep. I would tuck her little head into the sling, then I could do more sedentary activities such as reading and working on the computer. She would nap in the carrier or on my lap after nursing. She did not tend to sleep for long periods of time if I set her down, so I often found it easier to just keep going about my business while she slept. In fact, both of my babies often woke up when I tried to set them down (the dreaded transfer!) and would sleep better and longer if I just let them be in the sling.

As she got older, her naps got more predictable and I could wear her until she went to sleep, then I could gently set her down and she would finish her nap. As she got heavier, I found it a great relief to move her to my back with a wraparound or pack carrier.

Babies are marvelous creatures. They are active participants in babywearing. They will let us know when we get it right and when we goof. I remember when my son was about nine months old, he would let me know loud and clear that he did not approve of me setting him down at that particular moment. I would laugh good-naturedly, pick him back up, and reach for one of the many carriers hanging by our door. By the same token, as he got older, he would wiggle and squirm if he was held in a carrier for what he felt was too long. I would gently set him down so he could set off exploring. The short answer is – you cannot wear your baby too much, only too little. Simply do what feels right for you and your baby.

Choosing a Baby Carrier

Soft baby carriers can range from a simple piece of fabric wrapped around baby and mama to more constructed packs designed for serious hiking. The next four chapters review four major categories of soft carriers: Slings, Wraparounds, Front/Back Packs and Torso Carriers (for quick reference, please see OVERVIEW: Carriers By Style on page 94). For each category, I include a description of the carrier type; the main features and advantages of each carrier type, including ease of breastfeeding in each carrier; examples of each carrier type; and detailed wearing instructions. I have not attempted to include every carrier on the market. New carriers are being introduced every day. Rather, I have selected representative carriers from each category that I feel offer a unique feature or advantage. This is by no means a comprehensive list of carriers nor is the exclusion of any particular carrier meant to imply an inferior product.

You may wonder: what is the big deal about being able to nurse in a carrier? Remember, one of the main reasons so many moms love their soft carrier is *convenience* and nothing is more convenient than being able to feed your baby easily and discreetly while on the go. Plan to keep this in mind when selecting your carrier. There is some overlap between the categories and each carrier has its own set of advantages and disadvantages. There is no perfect carrier. My goal here is to review the rich variety of carriers and highlight the strengths of each carrier to help you find the carrier that best meets your needs.

Before we look at actual carriers, let's review some basic wearing tips that refer to all carriers.

General Babywearing Tips

1. All soft carriers should hold baby high and tight for maximum comfort and safety.
2. Baby should be rested and well fed before trying a new carrier.
3. Adjust carrier before handling baby, as babies tend to get very impatient with a lot of fumbling about.
4. While adjusting your carrier, try bouncing baby up and down (small, fast bounces) and shushing to soothe baby.
5. Once baby is safely in the carrier, get moving! Babies love the soothing motion. Try walking outdoors.
6. Be persistent: Try new positions until you and baby are comfortable. Observe how your baby likes to be carried in your arms and then try to duplicate that favorite position with your carrier.
7. Start with baby's head out of the fabric and plan to tuck it in when baby falls asleep. Many babies do not like having their head inside fabric.
8. General back wearing tip: Always lean forward while tightening the carrier to position baby high and tight.
9. Practice in front of a mirror until you feel confident.
10. Practice at home with another person if necessary until you feel confident.
11. Watch other experienced babywearers - at local La Leche League (www.lalecheleague.org) meetings, attachment parenting groups, the playground, etc.

Feel free to refer back to these tips as you get comfortable wearing your baby in various carriers. One of the biggest mistakes new parents make is giving up *too soon* on soft carriers. Because we often do not have real life models, wearing our babies can initially feel awkward. Babywearing is a *learned* skill that takes practice, and the best way to become an expert at wearing your baby is to *wear your baby often*.

Make Your Own Baby Carrier!

There are many prefabricated baby carriers on the market today, but please note: *it is not necessary to buy anything in order to wear your baby.* You may use a **simple piece of cloth** for a *tie sling, a wraparound carrier* or a *torso carrier.* For these less constructed baby carriers, you may already have what you need - a shawl, a large receiving blanket, a towel, a sheet, or a table cloth.

Your **simple piece of cloth** needs to be *three to five yards long*, at least *25 inches wide,* and meet this criteria:

- mostly cotton,
- breathable,
- resilient,
- washable,
- have finished selvage (finished edges),
- have a bit of diagonal give.

The fabric *must not be too thick*, or you will have trouble tying it. Cotton mesh fabric is wonderful. To test if a fabric is breathable, place it over your nose and mouth and breathe normally.

You need different lengths of fabric for different tying positions. A 2.8 yard length (2.6 m) can be used by most people as a tie sling. If you plan on using all wraparound positions, choose:

- 4.6 yards (4.2 m) if you are up to 140 lbs and 5'8",
- 5 yards (4.6 m) if you are up to 180 lbs and six feet, and
- 5.5 yards (5 m) if you are above 180 lbs and over six feet.

A shorter piece (about 2 x 1 yards, or 1.8 m x 0.9 m) may be used for a Short Cloth Tying torso carrier.

If you do not have such a piece of fabric already, simply go to your local fabric store with the above guidelines and buy the appropriate fabric. You may even use a rubber band wrapped tightly around the ends instead of hemming the fabric if you are pressed for time. Simply wrap the rubber band and then turn the fabric inside out. Making your own baby carrier from purchased fabric can cost less than five dollars and take five minutes!

(Please see www.mamatoto.org for more details.)

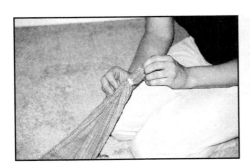

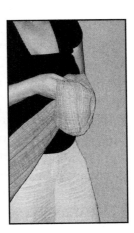

Hem fabric with a rubber band

Even the more constructed soft carriers (slings, pouches, packs) often have very simple designs you can copy with very few (if any) sewing skills. If you prefer to sew your own constructed baby carrier, please see the "Make Your Own Baby Carrier" section in the Appendix for patterns and resource.

Don't be afraid to try new positions and new carriers. Your baby will let you know when she is uncomfortable or when she has had enough. Let's review some basic safety information that applies to all carriers.

Babywearing Safety

1. Make sure baby is secure before letting go. Baby carriers are not meant to replace your hands; they are meant to give support while you carry your baby. Be ready to support your baby with your hands, especially as you are learning.
2. Check airflow around baby's mouth and nose to prevent suffocation.
3. Check baby's body to be certain that carrier is not cutting off any circulation. Pay attention to little arms or legs that are dangling.
4. If carrier requires you to tie a knot, choose a square knot.
5. Bend at the knees, not at the hip, or baby can topple out.
6. Have another adult help you with each position until you feel confident getting baby in and out.
7. Take special care around doorways and low overpasses as baby can get head or legs bumped.
8. Use caution with an uncooperative child. A child who is arching or wiggling could come out of a baby carrier.
9. Older babies can grab dangerous or breakable objects in a flash. Keep an arm's distance from potential hazards.
10. Wearing babies keeps babies toasty. Use care in hot weather, dress baby appropriately, and watch carefully for signs of overheating. Check baby often.
11. Wear baby cautiously in the kitchen. Take care near a hot stove or while working with hot or sharp objects.
12. Feel free to eat while wearing baby, but do not drink hot beverages when wearing baby.
13. Baby carriers should not be used in cars, airplanes, or bicycles as safety seats.
14. Do not use while climbing or using machinery.
15. Do not use while sleeping.

Babywearing in Any Weather

It is possible to wear your baby in almost any weather conditions. If you can be outdoors, chances are baby can be outdoors, too. In warm weather, take care not to overdress baby as your own body heat tends to keep baby nice and warm. Choose a lightweight fabric carrier such as a cotton mesh sling or wraparound. Apply sunscreen to any parts of baby's skin that are exposed to the sun and add a nice sun hat and sunglasses if you like.

In cold or wet weather, many babywearers have discovered that it is often easiest to put baby in the soft carrier and then put a nice warm (slightly large) coat or raincoat over you and baby. You can hold a large umbrella over both of you if it is raining. There are even specially designed overcoats and ponchos made to go over you and baby. The Felix Pera Coat from Germany and the Aiska Poncho from Finland are two great choices (find both at www.peppermint.com). For a wool poncho especially designed for babywearing parents with two head openings, try the Mamaponcho from Switzerland (www.mamaponcho.ch).

Wearing Baby on Your Back is Comfortable and Convenient

I have enjoyed moving my babies to my back as they get heavier. Small babies like to recline on the back while older babies usually prefer to be upright. I find wearing a baby on my back to be much more comfortable than wearing a baby on my front. Ergonomically, babies fit better on our backs. When they are upright, they straddle our hips and their little bodies fit the curve of our backs. We bear the weight better on our backs than on our chests. This is especially true for busty women who may have difficulty carrying baby close to their chest. We are not meant to carry weight straight in front of our chests; our back muscles strain under the unexpected weight. In many parts of the world, especially cultures where walking everywhere is the norm, babies are carried exclusively on the back.

When baby is on your back, you have both hands free in front of you. This makes tasks that require two hands, such as sweeping or doing the dishes, a whole lot easier. I have also found that wearing baby on my back makes bending-over tasks (such as emptying the dishwasher or doing laundry) more convenient. A baby riding in front is often in your way when you try to bend over. I find that I can walk long distances comfortably with a baby on my back. *If you have not already tried wearing your baby on your back, I would encourage you to try some of the back holds with the carriers we will discuss.* You will be pleasantly surprised.

Getting Baby onto Your Back

Many back carriers suggest or even require you to have a second person to load baby onto your back. This is a great way to get used to the feel of a baby on your back; however, this is not very practical for those of us who are at home alone with our babies. There is an art to getting baby onto your back without help from a second person. How you get baby onto your back depends on your personal preferences, the size of your baby, and the carrier you are using. With slings, you can load the baby in front and then swing the baby plus sling around to your back (see page 121). With the three other types of baby carriers (wraparounds, packs, and torso carriers), you have at least four options for placing baby on your back.

1. Start with baby on a sofa with the carrier underneath her. Sit in front of her and pull the carrier and baby onto your back. This method is great for beginners and is suitable for all back carriers. You may try this once you can prop baby up on a sofa (usually around six weeks or so). This method is perhaps the best place to start because it is the easiest to control and you have some cushioning for safety.
(For detailed instructions, please see page 155.)

  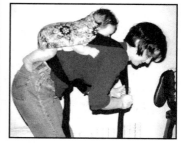

Start with baby and carrier on a sofa

The next three methods may be used as your confidence increases. We will start with the method suitable for the smallest babies.

2. Start with baby in your arms in front and gently roll her over your shoulder onto your back. As soon as she is over your shoulder, you should be holding her by both hands. Lean over completely to make your back a table. Once baby is on your back, you can wrap any type of back carrier around her. This method works best with younger babies, generally under a year. After that, they tend to get too heavy and too long to flip over your shoulder. (For detailed instructions, please see page 144.)

 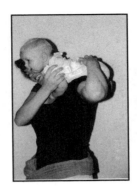 

Roll baby over your shoulder onto your back

3. Start with baby on your hip, lean forward and hop her around until she is straddling your back, then wrap the carrier around her. This method is great when baby gets too big to roll over your shoulder. You may try this method with wraparound carriers, packs, and torso carriers. Baby should be able to sit comfortably on your hip with good head and neck control (usually around four months) before you try this method. (For detailed instructions, please see page 166.)

Slide baby from your hip around to your back

4. Start with baby standing in front of you. Wrap the carrier around his back. Swing baby up and over your shoulder, like one shoulder strap of a backpack, then secure the wrap carrier around him. Because this method requires you to start by wrapping the carrier around your child, this method works especially well with tie slings (shown) and wraparound carriers. This method requires the most practice. It is a bit unnerving to swing your baby about like a sack of potatoes, but as you gain confidence and your baby knows what to expect, soon his movement will feel smooth and effortless. (For complete instructions, please see page 123.)

Swing baby up and over your shoulder

Look for tips on each one of these methods of getting baby onto your back in the upcoming chapters. No matter how you get your baby onto your back, you will love your new-found freedom!

OVERVIEW: Carriers by Style

Type	Description	Examples
Slings	Fabric goes over one shoulder and around the hip. Baby rides in folds of fabric close to the body in a variety of positions - front, side, and back. Slings can accommodate newborns to toddlers up to 35 pounds. You can change positions while baby is still in the sling, no need to reload. Most slings are 100% cotton, machine washable, but specialty fabrics exist. Slings are easy to put on and take off. You can breastfeed easily and discreetly in a sling. Adjustable slings are great because different people can wear the same sling. Also, you can loosen/ tighten while baby is in sling- great for breastfeeding- loosen for more space to nurse bigger babies. Pouches are tube-shaped fixed slings that are very easy to use. Pouches can't be beat for the in/out convenience, but it is difficult to do a vertical hold with a pouch. Hip slings are exclusively hip carriers, suitable for babies with good head control (usually around four months old).	**Slings with rings:** The Original Sears BabySling, SlingEZee, OTSBH, Maya Wrap, ZoloWear, Kangaroo Korner, TaylorMade Slings, Rockin' Baby Sling, Rosado, Moms in Mind **Tie slings:** Rebozo **Pouches:** *Fixed:* New Native Baby Carrier Chic Papoose Mamma's Milk Hotslings Kindersling Gypsy Mama *Adjustable:* Kangaroo Korner Maya Wrap Pouch ZoloWear Pouch MM Invisibly Adjustable Pouch Sling Baby *Hybrid:* Wise Woman Sling Baby Space Adjustable Pouch **Hip slings:** HipHugger The Hip Hammock Hip Baby RideOn Carrier

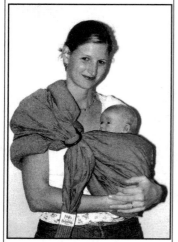

(page 97

OVERVIEW: Carriers by Style (continued)

Type	Description	Examples
Wraparound (page 131)	Long piece of fabric wraps around you and baby in a variety of comfortable positions - front, side - and back. All over fabric provides great support for newborns – adjust fabric up and over sleeping baby's head. Surprisingly easy to learn to wrap. Great relief to have baby supported on both shoulders. Best for distributing baby's weight. Not as easy in and out. Steeper learning curve. Breastfeed discreetly on both sides in front carry.	**Stretchy:** (easy in/out) Ultimate Baby Wrap Moby Wrap, Baby Bundler, Hug-a-Bub, MamaBaby **Woven:** (firm support) Didymos (bias cut) Girasol (bias cut) EllaRoo Gypsy Mama (gauze) Mama's Wings (embroidered) Kabuki (padded seat) Extra long Rebozo MamaRoo (fixed pocket)
Front/Back Packs (page 149)	Hold baby vertically, front or back. Hip carry possible, but not common. Favorite for back carry- both shoulders supported (unlike sling) and less fabric than wraparound. Breastfeed discreetly with minor adjustments in front packs.	**Fabric packs:** Kozy Carrier, Sachi Mei Tai, Baby Back-Tie, Packababy, Mei Tai, Onbuhimo **Constructed packs:** The ERGO Baby Carrier, Baby Bjorn (front only), Wilkinet, Sutemi Pack, Weego, Baby Trekker, 1st Journey
Torso Carriers (page 161)	Strapless back carrier! Fabric wraps around baby in back, under mom's arms, and over bust. Leaves shoulders free. Great for those with neck problems. Suitable for babies four months plus. Great for chores requiring bending over-loading dishwasher, laundry. Great for hiking and long walks.	**Short Cloth Tying** **Woven Wraparounds** Podaegi LoveWrap EllaRoo FreeHand Podaegi Hmong Baby Wrap

Chapter 5

*Slings: An Essential
Baby-Care Item*

DESCRIPTION

A sling is a piece of fabric that goes over one shoulder and around the hip like a Miss America sash. Baby rides in the folds of the fabric close to the body in a variety of positions: front, side, and back (see Sling Positions). In front, baby can ride vertically, facing in or out. While facing in, legs can be tucked up into the sling or left out for coolness and comfort. The vertical facing-in position is sometimes called the *Newborn Nestle,* the *Snuggle Hold,* or the *Tummy-to-Tummy* and is a favorite of little babies. This position is appropriate from birth on. The vertical facing-out position is also known as the *Kangaroo Carry.* For older babies with good head control, the Kangaroo Carry promotes visual awareness and is great for active babies. Both vertical positions are beneficial for babies with gastroesophageal reflux who need to be held in the upright position after eating.

Babies can recline in the sling, either with the head towards the rings for a very tucked in position (sometimes called the *Cradle Hold*) or with the head away from the rings which may leave the head peeking out a bit. This is a great position for nursing and is sometimes called the *Nursing Hold*. Both reclined positions can be used with babies from birth on. Although many photos of slings show baby's head towards the rings, this is not a preferred position for many babies. Many mothers who try this position report that baby fusses when his head is all the way in the sling. Positioning baby with the head away from the rings allows you to begin with baby's head completely out of the sling. You can always tuck the head in if baby falls asleep.

Babies who have good head control (usually around four months) enjoy moving to the *Hip Carry*. In the hip carry, always make sure the seat is lower than the knees for a secure ride. The hip carry is great for shopping and traveling because baby can observe the activities around him. Some slings can also be worn with baby on the back, in the *Back Carry*, once baby is old enough to sit up unassisted.

Slings are great for beginners. If this is your first attempt at babywearing, I suggest you begin with a sling. Slings are so wonderful, versatile, and useful, that if you ask me, every new parent should have a sling on hand. Slings should be handed out at hospitals and birthing centers as a matter of course. I have heard many an experienced mom remark that her sling is her most important piece of baby equipment. I heartily concur.

GENERAL FEATURES OF SLINGS

Most slings can accommodate newborns to toddlers up to 35 pounds, some a bit more. Most slings are 100% cotton, but specialty fabrics exist. Most slings are machine washable. One great advantage of the sling is that you can change positions while baby is still in the sling without taking baby out. You can breastfeed discreetly in a sling. If baby falls asleep while at home, simply lean over the bed, slip the sling over your head, and leave in place behind the sleeping baby, taking care that there is no loose fabric near baby's head (a suffocation/strangulation hazard).

| *Lean over bed* | *Slip sling over head* | *Leave in place* |

Sling Positions

Newborn Nestle **AKA:**
Snuggle, Tummy-to-Tummy
(Vertical, facing in)

Kangaroo Carry
(Vertical, facing out)

Cradle Hold
(Reclined, head to rings)

Nursing Hold
(Reclined, head away
from rings)

Hip Carry

Back Carry

All pictures used with permission

TYPES OF SLINGS

There are four main types of slings or one shouldered carriers: **Slings with Rings, Tie Slings, Pouches,** and **Hip Slings.** The first two types are adjustable at the shoulder through rings or by tying a knot. Adjustable slings are useful because different sized people can wear the same sling. If you are planning on regularly sharing your sling with a different sized person (dad, grandma, babysitter, etc.), it is convenient to own an adjustable sling. For breastfeeding moms, it is easy to gently loosen the fabric while baby is still in the sling creating more space to nurse bigger babies. Let's look at each of these types of slings in more detail.

Slings with Rings

Let's review the anatomy of a ring sling as shown in the diagram on the next page. The *rings* adjust the sling and sit corsage-level on your chest where you can reach them. Rings come in a variety of materials from nylon plastic to aluminum. The construction of the shoulder of a sling is a very important factor for comfort. Some slings come with a *shoulder pad*. Other shoulder styles include a pleated shoulder (material spreads out evenly across shoulder), a fanned shoulder (material is folded back and forth in a stacked manner with the top leaf often left free to form a "shoulder cap"), and a hot dog style shoulder (outer edges of the material are folded under towards the middle of the sling). Each shoulder style has advantages and disadvantages, and it basically comes down to a question of personal preference. The *rails* (padded or unpadded) are the top edges of the pouch where baby is placed, and the *tail* (sewn closed or not) is the extra fabric that hangs down from the rings. Ring slings are available either unpadded or with padding at the shoulder and/or rails. This padding usually consists of thin cotton batting. Tails can be either open fabric or closed fabric sewn together to form a strap. A *stopper* is sometimes added to the end of closed-tailed slings for additional security. Some ring slings come in sizes and the difference is the length of the tail.

Fully Padded Ring Slings: Fully padded slings have padding at both the shoulder and along both rails that is gentle on mom's shoulder and behind baby's head and knees. The padding is wonderful for bigger babies. I always enjoyed the gentle padding on the side of baby's head while in the reclined position. Some people like padded slings for nursing, feeling it stabilizes baby's head. The closed tail is great for one

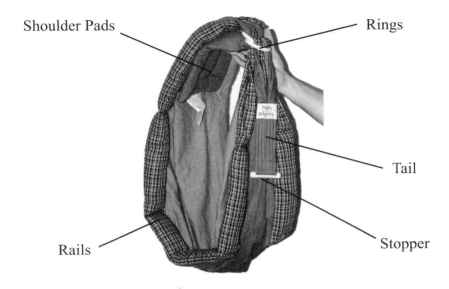

Shoulder Pads — Rings — Tail — Stopper — Rails

pull convenience. One major disadvantage often mentioned with padded slings is that the padding can interfere with pulling the top rail snug. For that reason, try to buy your padded sling on the small side. The padding can also make sliding baby around to the back position a bit difficult. Extra padding means extra bulk, and this can make the sling hot in warmer weather. **The Original Sears BabySling (NoJo)** (www.askdrsears.com) is the oldest and most well-known fully padded sling on the market today. It has marine quality plastic rings and a bar stopper at the end of the tail. The rings on this sling are unique in that they have *teeth* to prevent the fabric from slipping. This feature alone makes this sling stand out from the others. A sling that stays cinched tightly is a pleasure to wear. Other fully padded slings that borrow heavily from this original design are the **Sling EZee** (www.parentingconcepts.com) and the **Over The Shoulder Baby Holder** (www.babyholder.com).

> I love my padded sling! My baby spends most of her time in the sling sleeping and nursing. I can wear my padded sling for longer periods of time [than my unpadded sling] without needing a break; there seems to be less pressure on my shoulder. The padded rails provide a pillow for my baby's head and protection from the fabric cutting into her legs and leaving marks.
>
> Shelly, Texas

Spread fabric over shoulder

Unpadded Ring Slings: Unpadded slings are great because they are not bulky, and it is possible to cinch the sling very high and tight for maximum comfort. There is no padding to get in the way. This can be especially useful for the vertical hold and the hip carry. In the hip carry, it is necessary to pull the top rail quite tight in order to hold baby's body firmly against your own for maximum comfort. Unpadded slings can remain very comfortable even without the padding if you simply spread the fabric over the shoulder. A well-adjusted unpadded sling is every bit as comfortable as a padded sling, but it can be a bit more difficult to get the sling adjusted perfectly. If you find your unpadded sling uncomfortable, check that the fabric is evenly spread over your shoulder, that the sling is not twisted in the back, and that the fabric is not bunched up in the rings (this makes it difficult to adjust the fabric through the rings smoothly). Make sure you are carrying your baby high in the fabric, tightly against your body.

The **Maya Wrap** (www.mayawrap.com) is made of 100% cotton Guatemalan fabric and has an open tail which is great for discreet nursing and protecting baby from the sun. Some models include a Velcro pocket in the tail for essentials, perfect for keys or an extra diaper. A unique feature of the Maya Wrap is the shoulder cap. The fabric is designed to have a flap that you pull over your shoulder to prevent the sling from riding up against your neck. Many users find this makes the sling more comfortable. Several companies specialize in slings in unique fabrics. Most of these companies offer the traditional cotton fabric slings along with their specialty fabrics. **ZoloWear** (www.zolowear.com) offers heirloom quality silk unpadded slings that are spectacular. These beautiful open-tailed slings are perfect for a formal occasion such as a wedding. This sling also has a convenient zip pocket in the tail and a ring perfect for small toys or keys. **Kangaroo Korner** (www.kangarookorner.com) offers an open-tailed, unpadded Solarveil sling made of a fabric that can actually protect against sun damage. **TaylorMade Slings** (www.taylormadeslings.com) has an unpadded cotton mesh sling perfect for hot summer weather, an unpadded thermal sling made of a wonderful stretchy fabric that is gentle behind chubby knees, and an unpadded water sling made of quick drying nylon mesh. **Rockin' Baby Sling** (www.rockinbabysling. com) offers slings in linen and vintage fabrics with unique trim.

Beautiful silk sling

Custom Padded Ring Slings: Several companies offer a choice when it comes to padding, combining the best features of both padded and unpadded slings. **Rosado** (www.rosadosling.com) makes a sling that has "channeled padding" – basically light but dense padding which can be pulled through the rings, solving the design flaw of the limited adjustability of the fully padded slings.   With this lovely sling, you have all the comfort advantages of a padded sling plus the ability to pull the top rail snug.   It also has wider fabric than many other slings and is suitable from birth to 65 pounds (about 5 years old!), perfect for carrying older toddlers and preschoolers. **Kangaroo Korner** (www.kangarookorner.com) allows you to choose between no padding, light padding, or heavy padding at both locations, the shoulder and the rails, letting you customize your sling to meet your needs. The **Moms in Mind Sarong**

Carrier (www.momsinmind.com) is a lightly padded, batik sling with an open tail and a zip pocket.   This line of slings offers adorable matching baby clothes (www. bumwear.com), making a stunning shower gift for a special new mom.

Tie Slings

Some slings, such as the **Rebozo** (www.rebozoway.org), may be tied with a knot to fashion a one-shouldered baby carrier.

*Sling with matching
baby clothes*

Rebozo is the word used in Mexico for shawl. Many other cultures use shawls (or short rectangles of cloth) as one-shouldered baby carriers, but do not call them rebozos. I really consider these traditional carriers made from a simple piece of cloth – the rebozo, shawl, pareo, selendang, etc. – to be the *original* slings. Ring slings are actually very new. Traditionally, rebozos are twisted and tucked, not tied.

Tracy Dower
Creator of The Mamatoto Project, Inc.
Non-profit promoting babywearing

The absence of rings makes this sling the most versatile. When untied, the sling becomes a regular piece of fabric which can be used as a shawl, a baby hammock, a changing pad, or a place to lay baby down. In fact, you can fashion a tie sling with almost any type of fabric if you simply match the dimensions to your body. You need a piece of resilient, breathable fabric wide enough to accommodate your baby and long enough to wrap around your body. Make sure the fabric is thin enough to enable you to tie a secure knot. To test for breathability, place the fabric over your nose and mouth and breathe normally. In a pinch, I have used a throw blanket, a shawl, and a bed sheet. Some people prefer the tie slings because of their traditional appeal. You can enjoy all the same positions shown for the ring slings with your tie sling. Wearing instructions are the same: simply tie your sling first, then put baby in. Remember to tie a *square* knot for safety's sake. To adjust, you must take your baby out, retie the sling, and try again.

Pouches

Pouches are tube-shaped slings that are very easy to use. Pouches appeal to the minimalist in all of us. There is no extra fabric, no buckles or rings, nothing to adjust. Pouches fold compactly, making them perfect for slipping into a diaper bag or purse. These carriers are unique in that they have a *built in pouch*, unlike the straight hammock fabric of slings, so they are very secure. Experienced baby wearers use the term "popability" to describe how easy it is to "pop" baby into and out of the carrier. Pouches rate the highest on the "popability" scale. They are virtually hassle-free. Pouches are perfect for in and out of the car, and they are great for running errands. They are great for the up/down phase when your baby is learning to walk, but still wants to be carried sometimes. Leave it on, scoop your baby up, slide him around to the back when your hands are busy, swing him around to the front to nurse. Dads, grandparents and substitute caregivers tend to love pouches because there is nothing to adjust, making them feel very confident.

Pouches are often called the "training wheels" of baby carriers. It is difficult to go wrong with a well-fitted pouch. Put it on, slip the baby in, and go. There are few adjustments to make and, therefore, less to learn.

Darien Wilson
Pesident and Founder of ZoloWear, Inc.

Because of the minimal bulk, pouches are very easy to leave in place when transferring a sleeping baby into the car or onto a bed. If baby is sleeping, simply place both baby and pouch in the car seat, buckle up, and go. Lift both baby and pouch out when you reach your destination and slip pouch back over your head.

It is difficult to do either of the vertical holds with a pouch because you cannot pull the top rail snug enough (please note the Kangaroo Korner fleece pouch exception below). If you and your baby love the vertical holds (Newborn Nestle and Kangaroo Carry), consider using an adjustable sling for now and try a pouch as baby gets older and moves to the hip carry, usually around four months. The Hip Carry with

Easy to use pouch

a pouch does not hold baby's body in as tightly as an adjustable sling, because again, you cannot pull the top rail snug, but most people find the position to be adequate and comfortable anyway.

When selecting a pouch, think *small*: select a pouch that is small enough to hold baby up high and snug against your body, not dangling down by your hips. Fit is of the utmost importance when choosing a pouch. One of the most common mistakes is to buy a pouch that is too big and end up with a sore back and the feeling that baby just is not secure. Pouches must fit high and tight just like any other soft carrier. Do not be afraid that baby will outgrow the pouch just because it is snug. As baby grows, less and less of baby must be contained within the pouch. My daughter was in a size small pouch when she was two weeks old and today, at four years and 33 pounds, she can still ride in it. If you already own a pouch that is too big, you can make it smaller by simply sewing a straight seam at the top of the folded over pouch.

Fixed Pouches: Some pouches are simple loops of fabric that cannot be adjusted. They are available in different sizes to fit the wearer. These are the most compact, simple slings on the market. Dads and substitute caregivers tend to love them because there is nothing to adjust and they are simple to figure out. It is necessary to buy a sling for each different-sized person who is planning to wear the baby. In our family, we have a small pouch for me and a large pouch for my husband. Both get used frequently. The pouch is my husband's favorite baby carrier. With a fixed pouch, you can adjust the fit slightly with a "shoulder flip": simply hold the inner edge of the top layer (near your neck) and lift it up and out over your shoulder. This action pulls the outer rail tighter and helps hold baby more tightly against your body.

Popular fixed pouches include **The New Native Baby Carrier** (www.newnativebaby. com), which comes in a beautiful organic flannel fabric. This carrier is soft and sleek and is the ultimate in convenience. It has a built in hanging loop which is very practical, and the fabric is cut on a sharper angle than other pouches, resulting in a deeper pouch. It arrives tacked together at the shoulder which makes learning to wear it a breeze. (Please note: You will need to undo the tack if you want to do a shoulder flip). You will reach for this carrier again and again. I love it. It slips easily into a purse or diaper bag, and I always have mine with me.

The **Chic Papoose** (www.chicpapoose.com) is a reversible fixed pouch with beautiful prints on one side and coordinating solids on the other. The name says it all: the fabric choices are very trendy and the pouch arrives smartly wrapped. It is like getting two

pouches for the price of one. It is important to realize, however, that reversible pouches have *twice* the fabric of simple pouches, making for a heavier, stiffer carrier. Some wearers prefer this feel for a pouch, while others find it cumbersome. **Mammas Milk** (www.mammasmilk.com) makes a lovely reversible pouch with several unique features. It has a detachable "protection panel" (a Velcro-attached sheet of material that hangs from the front of the pouch that can serve as a nursing cover-up, a changing pad, a baby blanket, etc.), a built in diaper bag (a hidden flat pocket inside the pouch where several diapers can be stored), and padded rails. This pouch is very well-

Padded, stretch pouch constructed and has a polished look, with coordinating accessories such as a wipes holder and wet items bag. **Hotslings** (www.hotslings. com) also has the option of selecting padding in the rails. This unique option is great behind chubby knees and makes a great "handle" to get newborns in and out of the pouch. Their topselling fabric is a stretchy cotton (97% cotton, 3% lycra) pouch that gives gently and is a pleasure to wear. This is one very comfortable pouch. Hotslings also allows you to send fabric of your choice to be custom-made into a fixed pouch. **Kindersling** (www.kindersling.com) offers a beautifully hand-made cotton pouch. **Gypsy Mama** (www.gypsymama.com) makes a delicious towel pouch made of thirsty terry cloth, a perfect place to tuck baby after a bath.

Adjustable Pouches: Some companies are now making adjustable pouches for parents who want to buy only one pouch and use it for wearers of different sizes. These pouches can be resized before wearing, but cannot be adjusted while baby is in the pouch. In my experience, this option is great if you really have more than one person who will be wearing the baby regularly. This option is not really necessary for a growing baby or different positions. One of the most attractive features of pouches is their compact size. The ability to adjust makes the overall pouch a bit bulkier than fixed pouches, so make sure you really need an adjustable pouch before you buy one. Unless you plan to share your pouch regularly with someone of a different size, go with a fixed pouch. **Kangaroo Korner** (www.kangarookorner.com) offers a cotton adjustable pouch that snaps behind the shoulder and a fleece adjustable pouch that has wonderful stretch, holds its shape well, and is great behind chubby knees. Mothers have reported that the Kangaroo Korner fleece pouch is an exception to the rule when it comes to pouches and vertical holds. It is quite good for the Newborn Nestle hold.

The **Maya Wrap Pouch** (www.mayawrap.com) is an adjustable pouch cleverly designed with zippers and buttons. It is a generous pouch made of lovely, soft fabric. **ZoloWear** (www.zolowear.com) has just come out with an adjustable pouch. A single button and four buttonholes changes the size of the pouch. This clever design allows the wearer to button the pouch in several different ways depending on the need. The **Mamma's Milk Invisibly Adjustable Pouch** (www.mammasmilk.com) has a remarkable design which completely conceals the adjusting mechanism. One end slips completely inside the other end and is secured with a wide pad of Velcro, making an extremely trim, streamlined adjustable pouch. You may also choose padding in the rails. This pouch is available in a lovely stretch-cotton blend. The **Sling Baby** (www.

Sling Baby

walkingrockfarm.com) is an interesting constructed carrier made especially for young infants (7-22 pounds). It has a micro fleece, softly stretching, shallow pouch (especially appealing to parents of newborns) and a shoulder strap with a contoured shoulder pad. Baby rides in the pouch in front (no hip or back carry). The shoulder strap adjusts in back, before inserting baby. This carrier is designed to be worn on the left shoulder, but a right shoulder model is available at no extra charge. This polished, well-constructed carrier is a favorite of mothers whose young babies love to recline in a sling.

Hybrid pouches: Some of the newest carriers on the market are pouch/sling hybrid carriers. These exciting hybrids combine a deep, curved sewn-in pouch with the adjustability of a ring sling. Unlike the above adjustable pouches, these carriers can be adjusted while baby is in the carrier. A hybrid pouch has less fabric overall than a traditional ring sling. Because it is possible to tighten the top rail, vertical holds work well with these hybrid pouches (unlike traditional pouches). The **Wise Woman Sling** (www.wisewomansling.com) is an example of a hybrid pouch at its finest.

The carrier comes in a beautiful, soft flannel fabric with a generous, well-placed pouch. It has light, aluminum rings and a closed tail for one pull convenience. This is perhaps the perfect starter sling for parents new to babywearing. The seam provides a wonderful visual cue for where to place baby's bum and the closed tail makes adjusting the sling quick and easy. The **Baby Space Adjustable Pouch** (www.babyspaceslings.com) comes in wrinkle-ease fabric and has two toy loops and a pocket. It has an open-tailed design.

Hip Slings

Hip slings have a unique sleek design, but are largely limited to the hip carry. They are suitable for babies who have good head and neck control, usually around

Hybrid Pouch-
Great for beginners!

four months old. The **HipHugger** (www.thehiphugger.com) is a favorite because of its chic, sleek design. It is basically a pared down pouch, with only a wide stretch of fabric left for baby's seat. **The Hip Hammock** (www.hiphammock.com) is a bit more constructed with an added hip belt for carrying baby on the hip. It has a nice wide seat lined with butter soft fleece and a tall back to support baby. It buckles over the shoulder, has a great shoulder pad, and also buckles around the hip. When not in use, it rolls up compactly and ties right at the hip, fanny pack style. The **Hip Baby** (www.walkingrockfarm.com) adds an adjustable baby seat back and a contoured shoulder pad. It adjusts with a simple back slide buckle. It is made of climate control fabrics (micro fleece, mesh, and cotton). This is a very modern, well-designed hip carrier. The **RideOn Carrier** (www.rideoncarriers.com), formerly known as Sarah's Ride, is similar to The Hip Baby in design, but on a smaller scale: smaller seat, lower back for baby, smaller shoulder pad, and smaller straps.

| *HipHugger* | *Hip Baby* | *RideOn Carrier* |

For quick reference on these types of one-shouldered carriers, please refer to the Sling Comparison Chart at the end of this chapter.

Sling Wearing Instructions

Wearing Baby in a Ring or Tie Sling

When threading your open-tailed sling for the first time, please follow these easy directions:

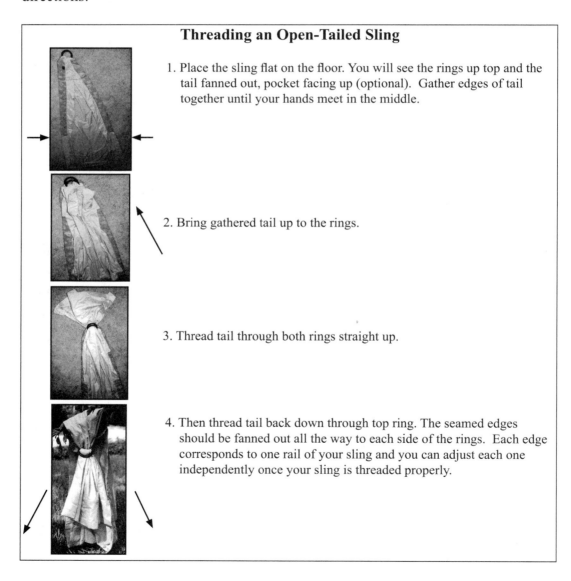

Threading an Open-Tailed Sling

1. Place the sling flat on the floor. You will see the rings up top and the tail fanned out, pocket facing up (optional). Gather edges of tail together until your hands meet in the middle.

2. Bring gathered tail up to the rings.

3. Thread tail through both rings straight up.

4. Then thread tail back down through top ring. The seamed edges should be fanned out all the way to each side of the rings. Each edge corresponds to one rail of your sling and you can adjust each one independently once your sling is threaded properly.

Make sure your sling is not twisted before you attempt to wear your baby. To test, put your sling on and run you thumb under each rail, front to back. In general, to tighten your sling, lift your baby's weight with your hand to "unlock" the rings, then pull down on the tail. Your baby's weight pulling down on the rings "locks" the rings and keeps the fabric from sliding through the rings. If you try to tighten the sling without first holding your baby's weight, you will only succeed in sliding the whole sling forward on your body. The sling will not tighten and the rings will end up too low on your front for comfort. To loosen your sling, lift up on the rings. Always hold baby's weight securely with your free hand while adjusting your sling.

To tighten a sling, lift baby's weight and pull tail.

To loosen a sling, lift baby's weight and pull up on rings.

If you are using a tie sling, put the fabric over one shoulder and approximate a knot so the fabric hangs just at hip level. Most tie sling manufacturers recommend always using a square knot for safety. You will need to test your baby with the knot in place and then remove your baby to retie the sling if adjustments are necessary. Many people find that once they find a good fit with a tie sling, they simply leave the fabric tied and lift it on and off over the shoulder. In general, you should not untie the knot while your baby is in the sling.

No matter how you want to wear your baby in the sling, all sling positions start with the same basic instructions on how to put on your sling. *It is a good idea to put the sling on first and get comfortable before picking up your baby.* When getting started, you probably want to leave your dominant arm free, so put your opposite arm through the sling. These directions leave the right arm free (baby rides on the left). To leave the left arm free, simply reverse these directions. Most sling manufacturers recommend wearing baby on both sides alternately for maximum back comfort.

Getting Started with a Ring or Tie Sling

1. Hold the sling, rings (or knot) in front, tail hanging down.

2. Put left arm through and lift over your head. Rings (or knot) should be corsage level. Sling should hang about hip level. Spread fabric over shoulder for maximum comfort. Run thumb under each rail from top, around your back to rings to make sure sling is not twisted.

3. Find pouch. Locate two rails, inner rail (always between you and baby) and outer rail. Each rail of a ring sling can be tightened independently by pulling corresponding fabric through rings.

Once you have your sling on, you can try several different positions. Let's start with a basic hold that most newborns love, the vertical hold, facing in with the feet tucked in. This position is called the Newborn Nestle, the Snuggle Hold, or the Tummy-to-Tummy position. If you can hold your baby over your shoulder, you can try this vertical hold.

The Newborn Nestle
(also called the Sunggle Hold or Tummy-to-tummy)

1. Put baby over free shoulder as if to burp her. Support with same side (left) hand.

2. Put right hand under sling and gather baby's feet together.

3. Gently slide baby into pouch keeping the inner rail close against your body. **Fabric must always be between you and baby.** Tuck baby's feet up into fetal position.

4. Pull outer rail up and over baby's back. May go all the way over baby's head if head support is needed-good for newborns.

5. **Tighten**. Sling MUST be tight in order to be secure.

6. Make sure baby is completely supported before letting go. Done! Start moving...

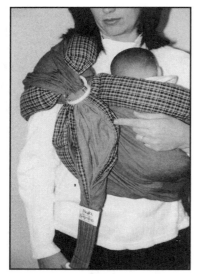

Isolate and tighten top rail
to form a "bubble"

With the Newborn Nestle, you want to make sure that the top rail is very snug to hold baby's body firmly against your own. You want to isolate and tighten the top rail. When you do so, the rail that you tightened will end up in a "bubble" if you are using a sling with a closed tail. Baby should be riding high and tight in this carry. If she is too low, or if her body sways when you move, you need to begin again and start with the sling pouch a bit smaller and higher.

Newborn Nestle, feet out

If she falls asleep in this position, simply loosen the top rail, pull it up and over her head, and tighten again to give her head support. As baby gets older, she may be more comfortable with her feet hanging out below the sling. As long as the bottom rail is snug under her bum, this is a safe way to carry baby.

As soon as your baby can hold up her head, usually around three or four months, she can enjoy her view when you hold her in the kangaroo carry.

The Kangaroo Carry

1. Face baby out and gather feet.

2. Open pouch and place baby in.

3. Make sure fabric is behind baby's back and sling has been tightened into a secure position. Done!

If you prefer to have your baby recline in the sling, you may follow the instructions for the Cradle Hold. This position is wonderful for tiny newborns. It is a very tucked in position, so older or more active babies may not like it. If your baby struggles or seems unhappy in this position, try a different position, such as the Newborn Nestle shown above, with the feet and head out.

The Cradle Hold

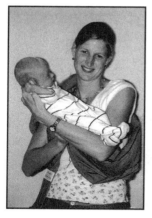

1. Lay baby across your forearm above the sling with her head supported in your hand. Your elbow should aim down into the open pouch of the sling.

2. Ease your elbow into the pouch. Fabric should be between you and your elbow.

3. Gently slide baby into pouch keeping the inner rail close against your body. **Fabric must always be between you and baby.**

4. Adjust baby's head into a comfortable position.

5. Pull outer rail up to make sure baby is securely contained in the pouch.

6. Make sure baby is completely supported before letting go. Done! Start moving…

Pouch Wearing Instructions

Getting Started with a Pouch

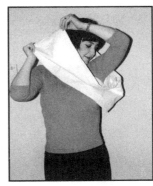

1. Start by folding the pouch in half lengthwise. Hold the pouch off to the side with the curved edge down, the tack (or the open edges) furthest away from your body.

2. Put your arm through and lift the pouch up and over your head.

3. You want to end up with the tack (or the open edges) near your neck.

4. Slide the pouch around until you end up with the seam where you want to position your baby's bum. Check in the mirror to make sure your pouch is not twisted around your back. The pouch should lie flat on your back and should be spread over your shoulder for maximum comfort.

Once you have your pouch on comfortably, you may place your baby in the pocket. Remember that neither of the vertical holds works very well with most pouches. (Exception: Many people like the fleece pouch for a vertical Newborn Nestle hold). You may want to try a shoulder flip (described above) to tighten the top rail and pull baby closer to your body if you do try a vertical hold. An easier position to try with a pouch is a more reclined position with a young baby or a hip carry with an older baby.

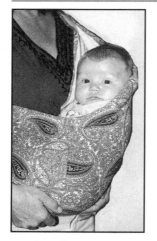

**Reclining in
a pouch**

When you are just starting out, it is helpful to have a second person help you. Hold the pouch open and let someone place your baby in the pouch. Remember, there should always be fabric between you and your baby if baby is reclining, and you should aim baby's bum directly at the seam. Baby may recline in the pouch facing either direction, either left or right, or he can straddle your hip for a comfortable hip carry. As you get more experienced, you can place baby in the pouch yourself by starting with baby over your free shoulder, opening the pouch and sliding baby in.

If you are planning to carry baby in the hip carry, hold baby against your body all the way above the pouch and pull both layers of the pouch out from your body. Let baby slide down your body, passing both of his legs through the carrier. On the way down, slip the inner rail of the pouch under baby's knees and then spread the fabric out for maximum comfort. In the final hip carry position, the fabric should start under baby's knees and end high on his back. In this case, there will not be any fabric between you and your baby.

If baby falls asleep, or if you need to nurse while baby is in the hip carry, simply gather baby's feet together and pull them to the front to lay baby down in the sling. Pull the extra fabric up over his legs for full comfort.

Ease baby into a pouch

Hip carry

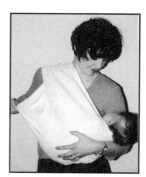

Reclined

Sling Transitions

Nursing in a Sling

One of the most wonderful features of slings and pouches is the ability to change positions while baby is still in the sling, which I call sling transitions. For example, if you are holding baby in the vertical hold and she falls asleep, you simply pull her feet to the side, lay her down, and tuck her head. You can use a similar technique if you want to nurse. There are many ways to nurse a baby in a sling, but this method is a good starting point. You can start with your baby in the vertical hold or the hip carry and follow these instructions to get her in a nursing position. Some mothers find it easier to nurse their baby in a sling if they sit down before beginning. Simply do what works best for you and your baby.

How To Nurse In a Sling

| 1. From vertical hold or hip carry, loosen rings. | 2. Lean forward, gather baby's feet together, recline baby's head away from rings. | 3. Latch baby on and nurse away. Retighten sling into a comfortable, secure position. Easy and discreet! |

You may also nurse your older baby or toddler in this nursing position, simply let baby's feet hang out the other side of the sling for extra room.

Newborns sometimes like to nurse in what is called the "football hold" or the "clutch hold." Tuck baby into the sling along your side with her head to the front, her feet to the back to nurse in the football hold. Some babies do not want to change positions at

all to nurse. They just latch right on from the hip carry. The sling can be loosened so baby sits lower to nurse in a hip carry. This is a wonderful way to nurse your older baby and toddler.

To breastfeed in a pouch, simply recline baby and slide fabric aside to allow baby access to the breast. Specially designed nursing clothes with slits are especially handy so you do not have to lift your

Nursing the older baby in a sling - feet out

Nursing in the Hip Carry

shirt. As baby gets bigger, it can sometimes get a bit tight in a pouch to nurse comfortably, but it is possible in a pinch.

Getting Baby onto Your Back

One of the most important sling transitions to learn is getting baby onto your back. This maneuver frees your hands and distributes baby's weight onto your back where it is easier to bear. You can wear your baby on your back in at least two ways, reclined or upright. Both of these methods work with ring slings, tie slings, and pouches.

Wearing your baby on your back in the reclined position works best with small babies who do not mind having their head tucked all the way into the fabric. This usually works best when baby is asleep. Start with baby on your front in the reclined position with her head away from the rings, sitting up with her head completely out of the fabric. I wear her around the house until she is content (or even asleep) and then I tuck her head completely in the fabric, grab the fabric behind her head and above her feet and slide the whole thing around to my back. Because her head started *away* from the rings (or the top of the sling, if you are using a pouch) in front, her head ends up slanting upwards in the back and she will sleep comfortably for a long time.

Back Carry - Reclined

1. Start with baby's head away from sling top

2. Tuck head in

3. Slide around to back

You may try the upright position as soon as your baby can sit comfortably on your hip and has good head and neck control (usually not before four months or so). Once you master this transition, you can start your baby in the front, slide her halfway around to the **safety hip carry** when you need two hands (for example, when you need to sign a credit card receipt) or when you need to keep baby's hands out of reach (for example, when you are cutting vegetables), then slide her all the way around to your back to walk long distances. You want the rings to end up above your bust or well below it for comfort. When she needs to nurse, just swing her back around to the front.

Back Carry - Upright

1. Start with baby in the hip position. Pull fabric high up on baby's back.

2. Lift back arm up and over baby's head to the front.

3. Put arm down in front of baby. This is called the **safety hip carry**.

4. Lean forward, and in a series of motions, *hop* baby around to the back, supporting her with your front hand.

5. Continue hopping her around until she is firmly straddling the middle of your back.

6. Stand up and tighten the top rail to hold baby flush against your back.

7. For maximum comfort, you may tuck the tail behind the rings for a bit of padding.

8. Done. Start moving.

If you are using a tie sling, you may prefer to get baby onto your back from a standing position. This method only works with a tie sling (or wraparound or torso carrier) because you need to start with the fabric wrapped around baby. You may try this method once your baby can stand unassisted.

Back Carry - Baby Starts Standing
Works with tie sling only.
May reverse instructions to wear on other shoulder.

1. Stand baby in front of you and wrap carrier around his back and under his bum. Center baby in fabric. Hold both ends of the fabric together in right hand and use left hand to support baby under his arm.

2. Supporting baby with both hands, swing baby and fabric up and over your left shoulder.

3. Take right end of fabric and lift over your head to end up over your right shoulder. Pass left end of fabric under your left arm. Tie a square knot snugly in front of your chest.

4. Arrange fabric so that it starts under baby's knees and ends high on baby's back. Done.

Maximize Sling Comfort - Avoid These Common Mistakes

Wrong

*Wrong -
Padded shoulder*

*Wrong -
Padded shoulder*

Rings too low

Make sure your rings are not too low - this is uncomfortable and makes the pouch smaller. If the rings are sliding down when you attempt to tighten the sling, make sure you are lifting your baby before tightening to "unlock" the rings

Fabric not spread over shoulder

A padded sling should be centered on your shoulder to keep the sling from riding up against your neck. Similarly, an unpadded sling should be spread out on your shoulder.

Right

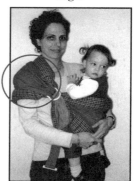

*Right-
Padded shoulder*

*Right-
Padded shoulder*

Maximize Sling Comfort - Avoid These Common Mistakes
(continued)

Wrong

Fabric twisted in back

Run your thumb under each rail from top, around your back to rings to make sure sling is not twisted.

Right

Wrong

Baby worn too low and too loose

Baby should be worn close to the body as high as possible. Notice the space between mother and baby. If necessary, isolate and tighten the top rail to hold baby firmly against your body for comfort.

Right

Wrong

Fabric bunched up in rings

The fabric should be spread evenly through the rings in a single layer - this allows the fabric to slide through the rings for easy adjustability.

Right

Sling Comparison Chart

Type	Brand	Comments
Rings- Fully Padded *Adjustable while wearing. Padding is gentle on mom's shoulder and behind baby's head and knees, but it can get in the way of pulling top rail snug. Padding makes back position difficult. Great for heavier babies. One pull convenience.*	The Original Sears BabySling (NoJo) www.askdrsears.com	*Beautiful design and fabrics. Has stopper at end of tail for safety.*
	The SlingEZee www.parentingconcepts.com	*Great for reclined position, padding is gentle on side of baby's head*
	Over The Shoulder Baby Holder www.babyholder.com	*Has ring at end of tail for safety*
Rings- Unpadded *Adjustable while wearing. Loosen for easy discreet breastfeeding or simply a position change. Can cinch very tight and high for maximum comfort. Not bulky. Comfortable with fabric spread over shoulder.*	Maya Wrap www.mayawrap.com	*Open tail, shoulder cap, Velcro tail pocket*
	ZoloWear www.zolowear.com	*Silk fabric- Heirloom quality, open tail, zip pocket, toy ring*
	Kangaroo Korner- Solarveil www.kangarookorner.com	*Open tail, Great idea! Blocks the sun's harmful rays*
	TaylorMade Slings www.taylormadeslings.com 100% Cotton mesh Thermal (cotton/poly) Water (nylon mesh)	*Very cool Stretchy fabric Quick drying*
	Rockin' Baby Sling www.rockinbabysling.com	*Linen & vintage fabrics, unique trim*

Sling Comparison Chart (continued)

Type	Brand	Comments
Rings- Custom Padding *Adjustable while wearing. Loosen while wearing for easy discreet breastfeeding.*	The Rosado Sling www.rosadosling.com	*Channeled padding pulls through rings for tight top rail*
	Kangaroo Korner www.kangarookorner.com	*Light/ heavy padding at shoulder and/or rails*
	Moms in Mind Sarong Carrier www.momsinmind.com	*Lightly padded, batik, open tail, zip pocket, matching baby clothes!*
Tie *Very versatile*	Rebozo www.rebozoway.org	*Traditional appeal*
Pouch- Fixed *Hassle free. No buckles or rings. Folds compactly. Secure built- in pouch* *Difficult vertical holds. Hip carry- Can't tighten top rail so doesn't hold baby's body in tightly like ring sling.* *Must fit well, not too large.*	New Native Baby Carrier www.newnativebaby.com	*Beautiful organic flannel. Soft and sleek. Ultimate in convenience.*
	Chic Papoose www.chicpapoose.com	*Reversible, prints on one side, coordinating solids on the other*
	Mamma's Milk Pouch www.mammasmilk.com	*Reversible, protection panel, diaper bag and padded rails*
	Hotslings Padded Pouch www.hotslings.com	*Padding behind chubby knees. Stretchy cotton fabric.*
	Kindersling www.kindersling.com	*Soft flannel fabrics*
	Gypsy Mama Towel Pouch www.gypsymama.com	*Terry cloth pouch perfect after a bath*

Sling Comparison Chart (continued)

Type	Brand	Comments
Pouch- Adjustable *Adjustable before wearing, cannot adjust while baby is in sling. Good for > 1 person.* *Ability to adjust makes overall pouch a bit bulkier than fixed pouches.*	Kangaroo Korner www.kangarookorner.com Cotton Fleece	*Rows of snaps behind shoulder Wonderful stretch, holds shape*
	Maya Wrap Pouch www.mayawrap.com	*Lovely design with zippers and buttons. Soft fabric, generous pouch.*
	ZoloWear Pouch www.zolowear.com	*Adjusts with a single button, four buttonholes*
	Mamma's Milk Invisibly Adjustable Pouch www.mammasmilk.com	*Hidden adjustment, stretch fabric, padded rails*
	Sling Baby www.walkingrockfarm.com	*Microfleece pouch with shoulder strap (7-22 pounds)*
Pouches- Hybrid *Sewn in pouch with the adjustability of a ring sling.* *Adjustable while wearing. Less fabric than traditional ring sling. Vertical holds possible.*	Wise Woman Sling www.wisewomansling.com	*Beautiful flannel fabric, well-placed pouch. Aluminum rings. Closed tail. Great for beginners.*
	Baby Space Adjustable Pouch www.babyspaceslings.com	*Wrinkle-ease fabric. Two toy loops, pocket. Open- tail.*

Sling Comparison Chart (continued)

Type	Brand	Comments
Hip slings *Unique sleek design, but mostly limited to the hip carry (4 months +)*	HipHugger www.thehiphugger.com	*Pared down pouch. Great in/out convenience. Sleek design.*
	The Hip Hammock www.hiphammock.com	*Wide seat with straps over shoulder and around waist*
	Hip Baby www.walkingrockfarm.com	*Adjustable baby seat back, contoured shoulder pad, climate control fabrics*
	RideOn Carrier www.rideoncarrier.com	*Same design as The Hip Hammock, but on a smaller scale*

Chapter 6

Wraparounds: Wonderful, Two Shouldered Support

DESCRIPTION

If you have never tried a wraparound, you are in for a treat! This is a long piece of fabric that wraps around you and baby in a variety of comfortable positions: front, side, and back. Wraparounds are probably the most versatile and comfortable carrier out there – especially for long outings with heavy children. Wraparounds do the best job of distributing baby's weight evenly over both of your shoulders and around your waist, but are a bit more involved to get on and off than slings or packs. This style of carrier has been used for centuries in many different cultures. The tie sling that we saw in Chapter 5 is essentially a short wraparound carrier tied with a knot at the shoulder. With a longer wraparound, there are at least four basic ways to wrap your baby: Basic Wrap, Simple Cross, Hip, and Rucksack. Baby can ride in multiple positions in each wrap-tying technique (for example, facing in or out, on your front or back). Each tying technique has a certain number of layers of fabric that go over baby, and you need a longer and longer wraparound the more layers you have. The wraparound is the original prototype that hospitals have used to care for preemies, wrapping baby and mother in the gentle folds of fabric and creating a human incubator/feeding combination in what is known as kangaroo care. When you are wearing a wraparound, it is like having your very own built-in pouch, the perfect place to tuck your baby whenever necessary.

The Four Basic Wraps

Basic Wrap
Three layers of fabric
Two crisscross, one seat
Seat can be in or out
Wear baby in front or back
In front: baby can face in (feet in or
out), face out, or recline

Simple Cross
Two layers of fabric, crisscross
Wear baby in front or back
In front: baby can face in or out

Hip Carry
Two layers of fabric, crisscross

Rucksack
One layer of fabric
Wear baby in front or back

GENERAL FEATURES OF WRAPAROUNDS

Most wraparounds are made of cotton or cotton blends. They are suitable for preemies to preschoolers. The all-over fabric provides great support for newborns and allows you to adjust fabric up and over a sleeping baby's head.

Wraparounds are surprisingly easy to learn to wrap. It is a great relief to have baby supported on both shoulders. Wraparounds are a bit more involved to get on and off than a sling, but the payoff is great. Wraparounds can do everything a sling can do and more. It is also possible to wrap in such a way to stay cool even in hot weather. Breastfeeding is easy and discreet *on both sides* with minimal adjustment in the front positions. This is a big advantage, especially with newborns who need to nurse often.

Pull fabric up over sleeping baby

I love the wrap style carriers! Prior to 3 months, we only used the [Basic Wrap] front carry. This is such a wonderful way to carry a newborn - it's so snuggly. I had at least one afternoon where she just slept and nursed in this position. We have done all kinds of housework (including sweeping which I can't do with a sling). We have used it grocery shopping and on an airplane. When she was really little, she could nurse on either side without really getting her out or changing positions much.

Michele, Texas

TYPES OF WRAPAROUNDS

Wraparounds come in either stretchy fabrics or woven fabrics (non-stretchy) and there are unique advantages to both. Stretchy wraparound carriers have a lovely bounce. With this type of carrier, you can put the wrap on tight around your body, then slip baby easily into the fabric. This is great for fussy babies. It is easy to leave the wrap on and take baby in and out. The stretchy fabric leaves more room to nurse bigger babies. When baby gets heavier, the stretch of the fabric can cause baby to sag a bit too low on a vigorous walk, so it might be time to switch to a woven wraparound. Woven wraparounds offer the support necessary for the popular back Rucksack carry. The Simple Cross carry is also better supported with the woven wraparounds.

Make Your Own Wraparound Carrier

The most basic wraparound carriers are essentially just a really long piece of fabric. I often get asked why it is necessary to buy a wraparound carrier at all when it would be so easy to go to the fabric store and buy a suitable piece of fabric. This is so true. There is absolutely no need to purchase a pre-made wraparound carrier. You simply need a piece of fabric that is at least 25 inches wide (0.6 meters) and meets this criteria: mostly cotton, breathable, resilient, washable, has finished selvage (finished edges), and has a bit of diagonal give. The fabric must not be too thick or you will have trouble tying it. Cotton mesh fabric is wonderful. To test if a fabric is breathable, place over your nose and mouth and breathe normally. You need different lengths of fabric for different tying positions. A 2.8 yard length (2.6 meters) can be used by most people as a tie sling. If you plan on using all wraparound positions, choose 4.6 yards (4.2 meters) if you are up to 140 pounds and 5'8", 5 yards (4.6 meters) if you are up to 180 pounds and six feet, and 5.5 yards (5 meters) if you are above 180 pounds and over six feet.

Stretchy Wraparounds

The **Ultimate Baby Wrap** (www.theultimatebabywrap.com) is made of cotton and 5% lycra and is the most stretchy of the carriers. It has rings at the end for looping through, but it is also just as easy to tie the ends. It has a built in front pouch and comes with a matching storage bag. While the bounce is quite comfortable with a young, light child, it makes it more difficult to keep the carrier wrapped securely with a heavier baby. The **Moby Wrap** (www.mobywrap.com) is made of 100% cotton jersey, like a thick t-shirt, a cool material that is very soft. It is wider than the Ultimate Baby Wrap so it is possible to do a secure back carry position. This is an ideal wraparound for a newborn. The **Baby Bundler** (www.babybundler.com) is also made of 100% cotton jersey material. The **Hug-a-Bub** (www.hugabub.com) is 100% cotton t-shirt material from Australia and comes with a beautiful instructional video. It has a unique front pocket that can convert to a built-in storage pouch when the carrier is not in use. The front pocket design is a visual cue when learning to wear the carrier. The ends of the Hug-a-Bub are tapered which makes for less overall bulk and easier tying. The **MamaBaby Sling** (www.mayawrap.com) is actually two unpadded slings crisscrossed that give the effect of a wraparound carrier. They can be used alone as a simple ring sling. The slings are made of 100% cotton interlock knit fabric. The MamaBaby two sling system is uniquely suited for holding baby high over the shoulder, a position many newborns prefer.

> Having a stretchy fabric makes everything I love about the [woven wraparound] 100 times better. This morning I had Violet (3 months, 13 lbs) facing out. When she started getting sleepy, I flipped her to facing in without much fuss since I could stretch the wrap over her legs to get her in and out. It's also easier to switch to a comfortable nursing position.
>
> Michele, Texas

Woven Wraparounds

Many woven wraparounds are offered in different lengths. When you are choosing a wraparound carrier, it is helpful to decide beforehand which positions you intend to use. The appropriate length of any wraparound baby carrier is based on your size and the carrying positions you want to use. In ascending order, the different wrap techniques need more fabric as follows: the simple Tie Sling (rebozo-length), the supported Hip Carry, the Rucksack, the Simple Cross, and the Basic Wrap which needs the longest wrap.

You may use the following guidelines to help you select the appropriate-length wraparound for your needs. If you plan on using all carrier positions, choose a wraparound that is:

- 4.6 **yards** (4.2 meters) – if you are up to 140 pounds and 5'8"
  (If you are long-waisted or large-busted, please choose the next size up.)
- 5 **yards** (4.6 meters) – if you are up to 180 pounds and six feet
- 5.5 **yards** (5.0 meters) – if you are above 180 pounds and over six feet

If you only plan on using your wraparound as a Tie Sling, for the Rucksack carry, or the Simple Cross carry, choose one size down from the above guidelines. In general, a 2.8 yard (2.6 meter) wraparound can be used comfortably by most people as a Tie Sling.

The **Didymos** (www.didymos.de) is made of certified organic 100% cotton that is cut on the bias making a carrier that gives gently but holds baby tight enough for the rucksack carry. The fabric is a medium thickness, about the thickness of a light blanket, and is very soft. The weaves are all reversible so both sides of the fabric look the same. The fabric is tapered on each end which makes it easier to tie the knot. This carrier is the ultimate in comfort and versatility. The **Girasol** (www.peppermint.com) is very similar to the Didymos, the fabric is cut on the bias and is a medium thickness, but the cotton is not certified organic, the fabric is not totally reversible, and the ends do not taper. The heavier fabric of these wraparounds makes them ideal for heavier children as they provide extra cushioning. The **EllaRoo Wrap** (www.peppermint. com) is a much thinner, more breathable 100% cotton fabric, but one which has enough strength to hold a heavy preschooler. This wrap is not cut on the bias so it is not quite as comfortable with heavier babies. You do have to take a bit more care to be sure that this thinner fabric is well-spread out especially with a heavy baby, but this carrier can be much cooler in hot weather. If you are looking for an even more lightweight, cooler fabric, the cotton gauze wraps from **Gypsy Mama** are wonderful (www.gypsymama.com). **Mama's Wings Wrap** (www.mamatoto.org) offers the option to custom embroider any message onto their cotton gauze wrap. This makes a wonderful gift for that special newborn. The **Kabuki** (www.rosadosling.com) is 100% cotton and has slight padding in the center of the fabric right where baby sits. The **Extra-long Rebozo** (www.rebozoway.org) is 100% cotton and can function as a wraparound carrier. The **MamaRoo** (www.mamaroo.com) is an interesting hybrid of a sling and a wraparound. It is basically a woven wraparound carrier with a fixed pocket sewn into the fabric. If the crisscross front carry is the position you use most, this is a very convenient carrier as there is no need to retie, just slip it over your head, drop baby in, and go. The two ends slip through the fixed pocket. When you pull, you get a drawstring effect that tightens the carrier quite effectively. You can also double it over to function as a simple sling.

For wraparounds at a glance, please refer to the Wraparound Comparison Chart at the end of this chapter.

WRAPAROUND WEARING INSTRUCTIONS

There are *many* ways to wear baby in a wraparound, many more than I will attempt to cover in this chapter. I will get you started with some of the most common ways to wrap the carrier, but please feel free to experiment and do what works best for you and your baby.

Basic Wrap

In general, with a stretchy wraparound, you complete the wrap first and then put baby in. With a woven wrap, you start the wrap, put baby in, then complete the wrapping process *over* baby. Let's start with the Basic Wrap. With this method of wrapping, you end up with three layers of fabric in which to support your baby - a horizontal "seat" and the two layers of a crisscross. Depending on how you wrap, you can finish up with the seat as the closest layer to you or the furthermost layer from you.

Basic Wrap, seat out   ***Basic Wrap, seat in***

Let's review the instructions for this first Basic Wrap ending up with the seat out. This works well with a stretchy wraparound carrier.

The Basic Wrap - Seat Out

1. Place center pocket against your stomach while holding ends with both hands.

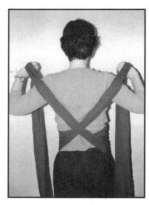

2. Cross in back and bring fabric up and over your shoulders.

3. Let fabric drape down on both sides.

4. Cross fabric in front.

5. Lift the center pocket panel (the seat) and pass all the fabric behind it. Pull cross snugly in front.

6. Tie in back. Or, you may continue to wrap the remaining fabric around your waist until the ends are short enough to tie.

To get baby in, you need to put baby in the cross and then pull the seat up and over baby.

The Basic Wrap - Facing Baby In

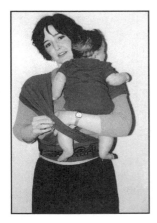 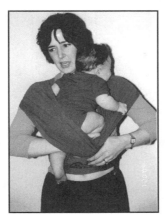 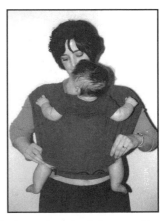

1. Place baby against your chest and pass his leg under the outer cross.

2. Lift his other leg and pass it under the inner cross.

3. Spread out both layers of fabric under his seat.

 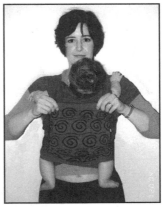

4. Pull the pocket panel all the way *down* and *under* his feet and then up and over his back.

5. Fan pocket panel over his back. Done.

If you prefer, you may wrap this Basic Wrap with the seat in close to the body. This works well with the woven wraparounds.

The Basic Wrap - Seat In

1. Place center of wrap across your chest.

2. Cross fabric in back and bring up and over your shoulders.

3. Let fabric drape down on both sides.

4. Place baby under fabric. Fabric should start at baby's neck and end behind her knees.

5. Cross fabric under baby's bum.

6. Pass the ends of the fabric under baby's legs.

7. Tie in back.

8. Spread out both layers of fabric under her seat.

9. Done!

With the Basic Wrap, you may face baby in or out. Baby should have good head and neck support before you attempt to face your baby out. With tiny newborns, you may prefer to place baby in the cross with her feet tucked underneath her. She may even prefer to recline in one of the sides of the cross. This is sometimes called the Peapod position.

Basic Wrap, reclined "Peapod"

Basic Wrap, feet tucked up

Baby can ride on your back using the Basic Wrap. With a stretchy wraparound, start with the center pocket against your back and complete the wrap in the same manner. You will probably need assistance getting baby onto your back once you have wrapped the carrier. If you are using a woven wrap, place baby on your back first, then wrap the carrier around your baby. If you need to get baby on your back without assistance, refer to the Getting Baby onto Your Back section on page 90.

Basic Wrap, on the back

Simple Cross

The Simple Cross uses only two layers of fabric over baby and one of the main advantages of this wrap method is that you can leave the wrap tied in a figure eight and then just loop it on each time you want to wear it. In the Simple Cross, baby can ride reclined, facing in, or facing out. If you prefer baby to ride on your back, you can wrap the carrier so the simple cross ends up on your back. There are many ways to wrap the Simple Cross. Here is one of the easiest:

The Simple Cross

1. Tie carrier in a loop then flip one end to make a figure 8. Hold behind your back.

2. Slip each arm into loop and put on like a backpack.

3. Grab a strap in each hand.

4. Bring first strap up and over your head to other side.

5. Do the same for the second strap.

6. End up with a simple cross on your chest.

7. Spread fabric out on each shoulder for comfort.

8. Place baby into cross, one leg thru each side.

9. Done!

Hip Carry

The Hip Carry uses two layers of fabric to support baby. You can tie this so you mimic a traditional sling (put the knot behind your hip), or you can add a hip support by crossing at the hip and continuing to wrap the fabric around your waist. Make sure to spread both layers of fabric over baby's bum for maximum comfort.

Rucksack

The Rucksack carry works best with a woven (non-stretchy) wraparound. You wear your baby in the front or the back in the Rucksack carry. You can get baby onto your back in several different ways. You begin with baby seated on a sofa with the carrier behind her, with baby in your arms, with baby sitting on your hip, or with baby standing. Review Getting Baby onto Your Back, page 90.

Hip Carry, supported

One of the easiest ways to get a small baby onto your back is to roll her over your shoulder.

Getting Baby onto Your Back - Roll Baby over Shoulder

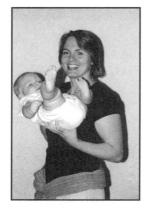

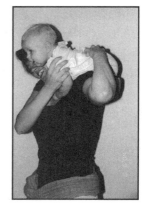

1. Loosely tie carrier around your waist. Hold baby in front, facing left.

2. Grasp nearest shoulder with right hand and place left hand under baby's bum.

3. While continuing to hold baby's shoulder, roll baby gently up and over shoulder.

4. Once baby is safely over your shoulder, switch hands.

5. You should end up holding both of baby's hands.

6. Lean over to make your back as flat as a table. From here, you can wrap any carrier.

Once baby is on your back, you may tie the Basic Wrap on your back or you may tie the Rucksack, as shown on next page.

The Rucksack

1. With baby on your back, drape fabric over baby from neck to knees. Reach your arms under the bottom edge and bring fabric directly up and over both shoulders.

2. Catch the bottom edge of fabric under baby's knees and gather both ends up and over shoulders. Twist the ends. Keep fabric taut. Here you have two choices, you can pull fabric straight back or you can cross in front and then pull fabric back.

3. Pass fabric *over* baby's legs, cross under her seat, go *under* baby's legs and...

If you prefer, you may tie a knot immediately under baby's seat in this step. Done.

4. Tie in front. Done.

Or try the Chest Strap Variation method of tying described below.

If you are not this adventurous, you may choose to start with carrier and baby on the sofa. To do so, place the fabric on a sofa. Place baby on the center of the fabric with the fabric starting under her knees and ending behind her neck. Twist the fabric on each side. Straddle her legs and sit in front of her. Pull both ends directly up and over each shoulder. Hold the ends tightly together in one hand. With your other hand, pull baby in close to your back and support her as you stand up. Remain leaning over and tie the Rucksack in the manner described above.

An alternative way to tie the Rucksack is sometimes called the Chest Strap Variation or the Tibetan. Instead of tying around your waist in front at the end of the Rucksack, you thread the ends through your shoulder straps and pull them snugly together in front of your chest. This serves as a makeshift "chest strap," a feature many more constructed backpacks already have. Many people prefer this method of tying the Rucksack because the "chest strap" keeps the shoulder straps from pulling back so much on their shoulders.

Chest Strap Variation of Tying the Rucksack (Tibetan)

1. Instead of tying the ends around your waist at the end of the Rucksack carry, pass each fabric end through the opposite shoulder strap from the inside to the outside.

2. You should end up with a cross in the middle and each end under a shoulder strap. Pull out firmly.

3. Bring ends together in front and tie a knot (or tuck ends in). The two shoulder straps should now be held firmly together. Done.

Wraparound Comparison Chart

Type	Brand	Comments
Stretchy Wraparound *Put on wrap first then slip baby easily into the fabric. Leave the wrap on and take baby in and out.* *Stretch of this fabric makes nursing on both sides easy and discreet.* *Lovely bounce but not as comfortable with heavier baby*	Ultimate Baby Wrap www.theultimatebabywrap.com	*Most stretchy wraparound, rings at the end, pocket and carrying bag*
	Moby Wrap www.mobywrap.com	*100% cotton jersey, wider fabric than UBW, ideal carrier for a newborn*
	Baby Bundler www.babybundler.com	*100% cotton jersey*
	Hug-a-Bub www.hug-a-bub.com.au	*100% cotton, tapered ends, contrasting, self –folding pocket*
	MamaBaby Sling www.mayawrap.com	*100% cotton knit, actually 2 slings that give effect of wraparound*
Woven Wraparound *Non-stretchy fabric* *Wrap partially, put baby in, then finish wrapping.* *The tightness of this fabric makes the back Rucksack Carry possible.*	Didymos www.didymos.de	*Organic 100% cotton cut on the bias, tapered ends*
	Girasol www.peppermint.com	*Cut on the bias, but not certified organic, no tapered ends*
	EllaRoo www.peppermint.com	*Thinner, cooler, breathable fabric, not cut on bias*
	Gypsy Mama www.gypsymama.com	*Lightweight cotton gauze*
	Mama's Wings www.mamatoto.org	*Cotton gauze, embroidered*
	Kabuki www.rosadosling.com	*Slight padding in the center where baby sits*
	Extra long Rebozo www.rebozoway.org	*100% cotton*
	MamaRoo www.mamaroo.com	*Fixed pocket, no need to retie*

Chapter 7

Front/Back Packs:
Soft Vertical Carriers

DESCRIPTION

Soft vertical carriers range from simple fabric designs to more constructed packs and are primarily for front or back use. Packs offer two-shouldered support (unlike the one shouldered support of a sling) with less fabric than a wraparound. In most packs, baby can ride vertically in back or front, facing in or out.

GENERAL FEATURES OF PACKS

Most packs are suitable for newborns up to toddlers with some adjustments necessary to carry tiny babies. Newborns are typically carried in the front carry. Because of the two shouldered support, packs tend to be a favorite for the back carry. It is easy to breastfeed discreetly with minor adjustments in the front carry with a pack.

Front carry

TYPES OF PACKS

The most basic pack is essentially a rectangle of fabric with a strap coming off each corner. The two bottom straps make the waist belt and the two top straps make the shoulder straps. Collectively, fabric packs of this sort are sometimes referred to as *mei tai* or *Asian Back Carriers* (ABCs) because of their Chinese inspired design. Fabric packs are sleek, compact carriers that fit easily in your purse or diaper bag. The more constructed carriers have the same basic design as the fabric ones, but have buckles and padded shoulders instead of the fabric straps. For the novice baby wearer, these tend to be easier to figure out. Some people prefer the constructed packs because the straps and buckles give them extra confidence as they are learning to wear their baby. Constructed packs can be a bit bulkier than the fabric packs.

Fabric Packs

The **Kozy Carrier** (www.kozycarrier.com) is an example of a simple fabric pack at its best. It is made of a wonderful, heavy-duty canvas-like fabric that makes the seat and straps very comfortable. There is very slight padding in the wide straps, and the top of the carrier is curved upwards to make a perfect head support for the tiniest babies. The fabric between baby's legs is thin and flexible allowing baby's legs to hang down so the back position does not force your baby to straddle your back (often impossible for small babies). The generous, firm head support allows even newborns to be worn comfortably on your back. The Kozy comes in a variety of beautiful fabric choices.

The **Sachi Mei Tai** (www.sachicarriers.com) has a similar design to the Kozy, but the fabric is more lightweight. The **Baby Back-Tie** (www.babyback-tie.com) has four long straps that are meant to form one single knot in the front. The **Packababy** (www.packababy.com) is similar in design and serves largely the same purpose, but the fabric is not quite as heavy. The look is not as polished as the Baby Back-Tie. The

Mei Tai (www.peppermint.com), imported from Asia, is meticulously embroidered resulting in a breathtakingly beautiful baby carrier, a true work of art. This is the lightest fabric and really works best with a lighter child (under 20 pounds) as the thin straps can dig into your shoulders when baby gets heavier. The **Onbuhimo Japanese Baby Carrier** (www.peppermint.com) has a slightly different design: it is a small rectangle of fabric with two straps at the top and loops at the bottom. To wear baby, the straps go over your shoulders, cross, go through the loops at the bottom and then around the waist. The Onbuhimo is a lightweight carrier and has a removable head support.

Constructed Packs

The ERGO Baby Carrier (www.ergobabycarrier.com) is a favorite for carrying older babies and toddlers on the caregivers back and is suitable for babies over five months old and up to 60 pounds. It is very easy to learn to use as simple waist and shoulder straps make up the whole carrier. Parents report that it is very easy to get baby onto their back without any assistance, a favorite feature with moms who are often at home alone with their children. This is one fabulous carrier. Serious hikers love the ERGO and report that it feels more secure than the metal frame backpacks they have tried. Perhaps this is because baby is held securely against the back closer to the center of gravity. The ERGO comes with a head flap that goes up and over baby's head when baby falls asleep.

The **Baby Bjorn** (www.babybjorn.com) is a very popular constructed pack, but it can only be used in the front. It can be useful when baby is still quite small, but it does not have the longevity of some of the other packs. If you like your Baby Bjorn, but feel like your baby is getting too heavy, you will love the **Wilkinet** (www.wilkinet.co.uk). The Wilkinet is a 100% cotton pack with a nice padded seat for baby and padded straps that can be wrapped to carry baby on the front or the back. It is suitable for babies 5 to 30 pounds. It is wonderful to be able to move baby around to the back as baby gets heavier. It has a nice, high padded head rest so even very small babies can be carried safely. It has no rings, zips, clips, or buckles. The Wilkinet works a bit like a wraparound, but with straps and loops instead of bands of cloth.

The **Sutemi Pack** (www.sutemigear.com) is similar to the Wilkinet, but it uses buckles instead of ties. It also has nice padded straps and is easy to learn to use. It helps to have a second person to get baby onto your back with the Sutemi Pack. The main disadvantage of this pack is that it must be worn with the straps crossed eliminating the rucksack style tie. The Wilkenet and the Sutemi Pack offer instructions for carrying baby on your hip which actually work quite well, but if this is going to be your primary carrying position, you would be better off considering a traditional hip carrier such as a sling.

The **Weego Baby Carrier** (www.weego.com) has a double pouch design that offers safe support for babies from 6 to 30 pounds. Baby rides in an inner pouch and an outer pouch zips up around him. Baby can ride facing in, facing out, or on your back. This carrier has nice wide, padded shoulder straps and is easy to figure out. This innovative company also offers the Weego Preemie, which can be used for babies from 3 to 30 pounds, as well as a Weego Twin, which can be used with twins from 3 to 15 pounds. The **Baby Trekker** (www.babytrekker.com) is the most heavy-duty of the packs and closes with a series of loops and clips. It is made of 100% cotton with extra wide straps with foam padding throughout. It is comfortable for babies up to 40 pounds. The same company offers a Baby Trekker lite, called the **First Journey** (www.first-journey.com) which is a bit more attractive and tends to make a better first impression on parents of newborns. It can only hold babies up to 33 pounds. Both offer the same carrying positions, but most people tend to prefer the backpack position of the Baby Trekker.

For a quick summary of all the packs, please see the Front/Back Pack Comparison Chart at the end of this chapter.

PACK WEARING INSTRUCTIONS

To get started with a fabric pack, first hold the carrier in front of you with the design side facing away from you and decide which is the top and bottom. Some carriers have the straps coming off straight and others use a 45° angle. Some fabric carriers have a distinctive curve at the top, while others are perfectly straight across the top. The bottom straps go around your waist and the top straps go over your shoulders. The waist straps are often shorter than the shoulder straps. If you are unsure as to how to orient your pack, please refer to the photo instructions included with your baby carrier.

Getting Started with a Fabric Pack - Front Carry

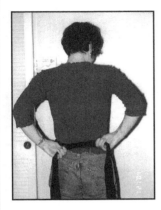

1. Wrap the bottom straps around your waist. Tie in back. Let the square of fabric hang down in front.

2. Hold baby to your chest and help baby straddle your waist. With the other hand, lift flap up between baby's legs.

3. Pull straps upward until snug and pull over each shoulder.

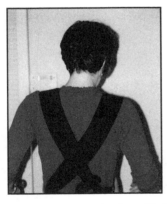

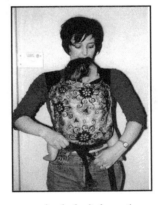

4. Cross straps across your back and bring forward under baby's legs.

5. Tie straps under baby's bum (or across baby's back for a smaller baby). If you do not want a knot in front, cross in front and tie in back.

Even the smallest newborn can be carried in these fabric packs in the front position. You may prefer to tie the final knot around baby's back instead of under the bum to help hold baby firmly to your body.

Babies often do not like their heads to be completely covered. If your baby is sitting pretty low in your fabric pack and he cannot see out or he seems uncomfortable, you may want to shorten the body of the carrier by rolling the bottom of the carrier *before* putting it on. This will allow your baby to sit higher up in the carrier, either on your front or on your back.

You can also carry your baby facing out in the front. Baby's legs are crossed in front of her body. Make sure to support your baby adequately in this position when you are learning.

Newborn in a fabric pack. Knot tied behind baby's back

To wear your baby in front in a constructed pack, follow the same basic instructions as for the fabric pack, but instead of fabric straps, you will have padded shoulder and waist straps. Simply tie or buckle carrier according to package instructions. The result will look very similar to the fabric pack instructions.

Roll pack to shorten

To wear your baby on your back in a pack, you have several choices as to how to get baby there. You may ask a second person to help you place your baby on your back. This is a good idea if you are just starting out and want to get the feel of wearing baby on your back.

If you prefer to work alone, you may begin with baby seated on a sofa with the carrier behind her, with baby in your arms, with baby sitting on your hip, or with baby standing (please review Getting Baby onto Your Back, page 90). If you are just learning, it is perhaps easiest to begin with baby on a sofa. It is easier to prop younger babies on a sofa than it is to slide them around from your hip. Instructions for getting baby onto your back starting with baby on a sofa are pictured in the next section. In this series, baby Harrison is three months old and Mom is using a fabric pack.

Fabric pack, facing forward

Fabric Pack: Back Carry - Baby Starts on Sofa

1. Position fabric pack - curved end up, shoulder straps up and over the back of the sofa, and waist straps straight forward.

2. Place baby onto pack - both waist straps *between* his legs. Baby's legs should rest *over* each strap.

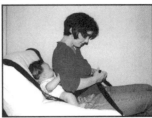

3. Straddle his legs and sit in front of baby. Pull waist straps up and tie around your waist. (Roll first for shorter carrier.)

4. Pull shoulder straps up and over each shoulder. Hold together in one hand in front. With your other hand, support baby's bottom.

5. Pull shoulder straps snug, slowly stand up, and lean forward. Baby is supported by tied waist strap and held by shoulder straps.

6. Lean forward so your back makes a table. Here you have two choices: cross the straps across your chest. or pull the straps straight back, rucksack style.

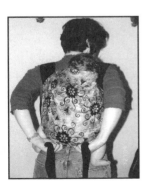

7. Pass straps under baby's legs and tie under his bum (or back). If you prefer, cross under his bum, continue forward, and tie in front. You always have the option to run straps *over* or *under* baby's legs. You may want to experiment to find the most comfortable and secure position for your baby.

A variation on the Back Carry with a fabric pack is called the *High Back Carry*. To do the High Back Carry, start by tying the waist straps above your bust instead of around your waist. The rest of the instructions are the same as for the normal Back Carry: put baby on your back, pull both shoulder straps up over your shoulders, cross in front, and tie in back. The High Back Carry allows baby to ride higher on your back and see over your shoulder. Some people find this carry more comfortable with smaller babies. Pregnant mothers also tend to like this carry as there are no straps near their belly.

Follow the instructions on the facing page to get baby onto your back using a constructed pack, starting with baby and carrier on a sofa.

Baby and carrier on sofa.

Once you can confidently get your baby onto your back from the sofa starting position, you are ready to try some of the other methods for getting baby onto your back. Baby may be moved to your back from the hip position, using either a fabric or constructed pack. This method requires practice. You should only try this method with a cooperative baby. Your baby should be able to sit comfortably on your hip without you needing to support her head or neck. When you are learning, it is a good idea to stand in front of something soft, such as a sofa or a bed. This gives baby some cushioning for extra safety in case she needs it.

Constructed Pack: Back Carry
Baby Starts on Sofa

1. Place constructed pack on sofa.

2. Place baby onto pack, bottom strap behind baby's knees.

3. Straddle baby's legs and sit in front of her. Pull up shoulder straps.

4. Hold shoulder straps together in front hand. Support baby with other hand. Lean forward, stand up, and tie carrier. Remain leaning over until baby is securely tied.

5. Done.

Back Carry - Baby Starts on Hip

1. Put on the pack as usual and fasten (or tie) the waist belt.

2. Drop your right arm strap behind your back. (Let fabric packs hang down in back.)

3. Hold baby on your right hip.

4. Pull baby's left foot through the constructed pack on the back.

5. Lean forward, support baby with back hand, and in a series of motions, *hop* baby around to the back until she is straddling the middle of your back.

6. While still leaning forward, pull right strap back up over shoulder.

7. Check baby's position to make sure she is secure.

8. Click chest strap (some constructed packs).

9. Done! Start moving…

Front/Back Pack Comparison Chart

Type	Brand	Comments
Fabric Pack *Rectangle of fabric with a strap coming off each corner. Sleek and compact.*	Kozy Carrier www.kozycarrier.com	*Heavy duty canvas fabric, slightly padded straps, top curved upwards for head support*
	Sachi Mei Tai www.sachicarriers.com	*Lightweight fabric*
	Baby Back-Tie www.babyback-tie.com	*Forms single knot in front*
	Packababy www.packababy.com	*Lighter fabric*
	Mei Tai www.peppermint.com	*Thinnest fabric. Intricate embroidery. Best for lighter child*
	Onbuhimo www.peppermint.com	*Rings, not straps, at bottom of carrier. Lightweight with head support*
Constructed Pack *Same basic design as fabric packs, but have buckles and padded shoulders instead of fabric straps. Bulkier, but may inspire confidence.*	The ERGO Baby Carrier www.ergobabycarrier.com	*Buckles and clips. Head flap for sleeping baby*
	Baby Bjorn www.babybjorn.com	*Front carry only*
	Wilkinet www.wilkinet.co.uk	*Straps and loops. Front and back carry. High padded head rest*
	Sutemipack www.sutemigear.com	*Buckles and snaps. No rucksack tie*
	Weego Baby Carrier www.weego.com	*Double pouch. Preemie & Twin models*
	Baby Trekker www.babytrekker.com	*Heavy duty. Loops and clips*
	First Journey www.first-journey.com	*Up to 33 lbs.*

Chapter 8

Torso Carriers:
Strapless Back Carriers

DESCRIPTION

Back torso carriers consist of a piece of fabric that wraps around baby on the back, goes under the caregiver's arms and over the bust, and ties in front, or wraps to tie in back. This type of carrier leaves the shoulders completely free and is great for those with neck problems. Baby rides sitting upright on the back, or less commonly, on the front.

GENERAL FEATURES OF TORSO CARRIERS

Back torso carriers are only suitable for babies with good head and neck control, usually around four months or so. They are great for chores that require bending or reaching overhead such loading and emptying the dishwasher or doing laundry. They are so comfortable that they are a favorite for hiking and long walks.

Many worry that it is necessary to be quite busty to "hold" the carrier up, but rest assured that anyone can hold a baby this way. In many places, older siblings who

Short cloth tying

have not even hit puberty carry their younger brother or sister in this fashion. Some nursing mothers find it uncomfortable to have pressure above the breasts, but I have never minded and find these back torso carriers to be wonderfully freeing. If you are prone to plugged ducts or mastitis, it is a good idea to pay attention to this area when using a torso carrier.

TYPES OF TORSO CARRIERS

The simplest back torso carrier is a relatively short piece of fabric tied above the breasts and around the waist, what I call **Short Cloth Tying**. Over the holidays, we had an exchange student from Senegal come stay with us. She took one look at our two-month-old son and asked if she could put him on her back. Elisabeth took a piece of thin cotton fabric that I was planning to use to cover a sofa pillow and proceeded to expertly tie our son to her back, with one knot chest level and one knot waist level. She explained that in Senegal, women use a short piece of breathable, resilient fabric (approximately 2 yards by 1 yard wide) to tie babies to their back. I carried our baby in this manner for many months and found that the most comfortable way to carry him was high and tight on my back.

Front torso carry

This Senegalese cloth tying method fastens baby to your back with a relatively short piece of fabric that is knotted in two places in front, above the chest and at waist level. If you prefer a longer piece of fabric, you can use any of the woven wraparound carriers mentioned in the Wraparound chapter (Chapter 6) or a piece of purchased fabric. Simply keep wrapping the fabric around you and baby until you reach the end, then tuck the ends under. You may wear your baby in the front in this manner, also.

A *podaegi* is a traditional baby carrier design from Korea comprised of a quilt-like piece of rectangular fabric (blanket) that has long straps attached to the top two corners. This is a lovely comfortable carrier that I love wearing during the colder months here in Texas.

LoveWrap (www.lovewrap.com) offers a beautiful, custom-made podaegi with either the traditional wide blanket or a more narrow blanket design and straps that are padded with light batting or foam. The wide blanket with thin batting is more comfortable for the traditional strapless torso hold and some mothers prefer the wide blanket because of the swaddling effect of wrapping baby in the full blanket.

Wide blanket podaegi

Their most popular style of podaegi, however, is the narrow blanket with foam padded straps. The foam padding makes this carrier more comfortable when used with heavier babies and toddlers. The narrow blanket design is cooler and allows

Swaddling effect of a podaegi

more freedom of movement for an older child. The **EllaRoo Podaegi** (www.peppermint.com) also comes in a wide or narrow blanket design. The FreeHand Podaegi (www.freewebs. com/freehand) can be made to order with either straight or angled straps and a narrow or wide blanket. FreeHand also offers a unique FreeHand Hmong carrier (www.freewebs.com/freehand) which is similar to the podaegi, but instead of a single piece of fabric in the back, it is made up of two rectangles

of fabric stitched together, one stacked above the other. A small, thick rectangle of fabric makes up the upper part of the carrier. It has the straps coming off either side and a wider, thinner rectangle of fabric hangs directly below it. The Hmong is worn in the same manner as the podaegi. Although it is most common to use the podaegi for the back torso hold, it is possible to wear the podaegi with the straps *over* the shoulders for a pack-like carrier option.

Baby Wrap

The **Baby Wrap** (www.babywrapinc.com) is the most structured of the torso carriers. It is basically a soft, strapless baby carrier with a sewn in baby seat. As far as I can tell, the baby seat is largely unnecessary as baby is held firmly against the back, but some parents like the extra feeling of security. There is a strap that buckles over the bust and a fabric sash that ties at the waist. This carrier has a firm back to give support for small babies.

For quick reference, please see the Torso Carrier Comparison Chart at the end of this chapter.

TORSO CARRIER WEARING INSTRUCTIONS

In this section, I will provide torso carrier instructions for wearing baby on the back. Although it is possible to wear your baby in the front using a torso carrier, this is not very common and other carriers are perhaps better suited for the front carry. As with wearing baby on the back with Wraparounds and Packs, you again have several options as to how you want to begin. You may begin with baby seated on a sofa with the carrier behind her, with baby in your arms, with baby sitting on your hip, or with baby standing (please review Getting Baby onto Your Back, page 90). In this series, we will get baby onto the back by rolling her over mom's shoulder, and we will secure her with a purchased length of fabric, essentially a woven wraparound.

Torso Carry with a Wraparound

1. Loosely tie carrier around your waist. Hold baby in front, facing left.

2. Grasp nearest shoulder with right hand and place left hand under baby's bum.

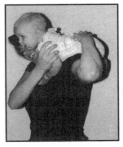

3. While continuing to hold baby's shoulder, roll baby gently up and over shoulder.

4. Once baby is safely over your shoulder, switch hands.

5. You should end up holding both of baby's hands.

6. Lean over to make your back as flat as a table. From here, you may wrap any carrier.

7. Pull fabric up to baby's neck and snugly under baby's knees.

8. Cross fabric in front, over bust, then toss each end back around the back. Cross ends under baby's bum.

9. Tie in front. Done.

In the next series, we will start with baby on mama's hip and end up with her secured on the back in a torso carry using a wide blanket Podeagi. If you prefer to carry baby using the over-the-shoulder method, you may run the straps over your shoulders after crossing in front.

Torso Carry with a Podaegi

1. Start with baby far back on your hip.

2. Hold baby with your front arm. Lean to the side and slightly forward. Lift your back arm up and over baby's head to the front.

3. Lean completely over and hop baby around until she is straddling your back. Hold baby with both hands.

4. Drape podaegi over baby's back. Top edge should be at baby's neck.

5. Remain leaning over and cross straps snugly in front, over bust. (Shoulder carry: cross straps in front then go over shoulders.)

6. Run straps *over* baby's legs to the back and cross straps under baby's bum.

7. Tie in front.

8. Done.

Torso Carrier Comparison Chart		
Type	**Brand**	**Comments**
Torso carriers *Strapless back carriers, leave shoulders free.*	Short Cloth Tying	*Relatively short cloth (2 x 1 yards) tied above chest and at waist. Simplest method - purchase cloth at your local fabric store.*
	Woven Wraparounds	*See Chapter 6*

	Podaegi
	    LoveWrap
	    www.lovewrap.com
	    EllaRoo
	    www.peppermint.com
	    FreeHand Podaegi
	    www.freewebs.com/freehand
	    FreeHand Hmong
	    www.freewebs.com/freehand
		Quilted rectangle with long straps at top. Wide or narrow blanket. Very comfortable. Over the shoulder carry possible.

	Baby Wrap www.BabyWrapInc.com	*Sewn-in baby seat. Firm back support.*

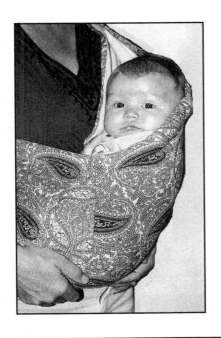

Chapter 9

Frequently Asked Questions

Choosing a Carrier

I am a new first time mother and my daughter is five weeks old. I am interested in wearing my baby, but I am not sure where to begin. Money is a bit tight so I need to select a carrier carefully. If I were to choose only one carrier, which one should I buy?

Since money is tight, you may want to consider making a carrier out of a simple piece of cloth you may already have at home. More information can be found in this book in the "Make Your Own Baby Carrier" section on page 86. In this way, you and your baby can try out babywearing and get an idea of what works for you before you spend any money.

As for choosing a single carrier to meet all your needs, there is no easy answer.

I often compare baby carriers to shoes. Most people have at least several pairs of shoes for different purposes. Like shoes, slings are worn for hours at a time and need to be comfortable. Sometimes, quick on and off is the feature most needed. Sometimes, temperature is a factor so one chooses a sling that is cool in hot weather or cozy in chilly weather. Sometimes, one chooses a carrier that is suitable for exercise walks or one that looks nice with dressier clothes. I often find that folks can use about three different carriers to meet most or all of their needs from newborn until three or more years.
Terrie Abrahamson
Independent Babywearing Consultant

Plan to review all the options in this book and try to decide which features are most important to you. Although you could *use* several different carriers throughout your babywearing years, you certainly do not *need* several carriers. Many moms choose to invest in several carriers once they realize how much they use their carriers. Sometimes, it is just a question of priorities: if you use your baby carrier every day, you may feel comfortable spending money that you might have spent on lesser-used baby equipment. As new parents, we often do not bat an eye at spending large sums of money on popular baby holders such as bouncy chairs, infant swings, bassinets, or cribs. Many new parents find that their baby hardly uses these items, preferring instead the loving security of a soft baby carrier. A good plan is to resist the urge to buy many big-ticket items before or as soon as baby is born. Instead, try each item at the store or at a friend's house to be sure baby really likes it. Use the money you save to put towards the carrier or carriers of your choice.

That said, a good starting point for all new parents interested in babywearing is a sling. You cannot go wrong with a basic cotton sling. Slings are relatively easy to learn to use, and they are extremely versatile. With a sling alone, you can easily carry your newborn daughter from birth until she is three or four years old. For a great starter sling, try one of the pouch hybrids with a closed tail. This sling is one of the easiest baby carriers to learn to use, and it is extremely comfortable and versatile.

Lifespan of Soft Baby Carriers

I have just bought my first sling for my newborn daughter, and I am wondering how long I will be able to continue to use it with her? Will she outgrow it soon?

A soft baby carrier is without a doubt one of the best investments you will make.

While the lifespan of many baby items can be measured in terms of *months*, most parents use their soft baby carriers for *years*.

Most soft baby carriers can safely be used from birth until about 35 pounds. Check the instructions that come with your particular model for details. One of the beautiful things about soft baby carriers is that most babies outgrow the *need* before they outgrow the *carrier*. In my experience, this has been the typical course of babywearing: constant for the first twelve months or so; less as baby moves into toddlerhood and wants to be down; and sporadically as baby leaves toddlerhood behind. You may wear your older baby/toddler when she is tired, sick, or for safety reasons when it makes sense to keep baby close: for example, in the airport, a parking lot, or a large state fair. You can look forward to enjoying many years of wearing your baby.

Babywearing and "Spoiling"

My six-month-old son loves his sling! I love the ease of carrying him, and he is contented and easy when he is in the sling. My mother says that I am spoiling him by carrying him all the time. I feel right carrying him, but I worry that my mother may have a point.

Although it is common to worry that we will "spoil" our babies by meeting their needs, this has never been proven to be true. Babies have a biological need to be close to their caregivers and that need persists to early childhood, whether we carry our babies or not. By meeting the needs of your baby early on, you are setting him up for a lifetime of feeling secure and attached. Trust your baby to tell you exactly how much holding he needs and follow his cues.

Parents often fear that they will create a "dependent" baby by holding their baby often. They worry that their baby will become whiney and demanding. I have noticed that the opposite is actually true. Babies who consistently have their need for closeness met early on enjoy a sense of well-being that allows them to venture forth in the world with confidence and trust. A need that is met goes away. All babies are, by their very nature, "dependent." They cannot survive without us. We just decide on what they will depend. Yes, babies who are held close do in fact become dependent on human touch, but babies who are not held close become "dependent" as well. In my experience, babies who are denied closeness are often the ones who end up "dependent" on non-human things (special toys, pacifiers, bottles, wind-up swings, etc.). For a baby to become dependent on human beings instead of *things* is certainly not a bad thing in my book! Human beings are the original "pacifiers," the world's most perfect, effective baby-soothers. Other things are the imitations, the never quite perfect substitutes.

Each generation (and each parent) tries to do what is best for our children with the information we have available at the time. Choosing to do things differently from your mother is not a negative reflection on your mother's mothering. Instead, it is a proactive, deliberate attempt on your part to do what you think is best for your child. You are, after all, the expert on your baby and know what is best for him.

Babywearing and Sleep Habits

I have a three-month-old daughter who pretty much lives in her sling. Although I am most impressed with how easy life is with a sling baby, I have some persistent doubts. My older daughters had strict nap schedules by the time they were this age. I am worried that by wearing my baby during her naps, I am creating bad sleep habits that I may regret later on.

Babies are remarkably resilient, they can thrive with all sorts of caregiving. You are already giving your daughter exactly what she needs by holding her close. She is still very young, and it makes sense that she would often sleep in the sling during the day. There is actually an advantage to wearing her often as babywearing during the day has been shown to help babies sleep better at night (see Chapter 1).

There is no need to worry that you are creating "bad habits." If you choose to start putting your baby down for her naps, she will likely adjust to this as the norm. If you continue to hold her during her naps, she will likely love this as well. In fact, being able to wear your baby to sleep is often cited as an extremely valuable parenting tool, making baby portable even during naptimes. While we can certainly create a sleep-conducive environment, there is no way we can ever *make* a baby sleep. All over the world, babies get the sleep they need without benefit of so-called "sleep training." Do what feels right for you and your baby and trust that as she grows your baby will let you know how her needs are changing.

Babywearing and Developmental Milestones

I love wearing my four-month-old, but my father-in-law keeps warning me that if I wear him all the time, he will never learn to walk. I also keep hearing that babies need "tummy time," and I am concerned that he won't get enough tummy time if I am carrying him all the time. Am I really doing the right thing?

Rest assured that wearing your baby will not delay his normal developmental milestones. In fact, all evidence points to the contrary: carried babies develop *better* than stationary babies (see Chapter 1). Babywearing activates baby's vestibular system (used for balance) and encourages him to use his head and neck muscles to compensate for your movements. Because of this, the time that you wear your baby can actually count as "tummy time."

Babywearing is not a passive activity. Your baby is an active partner and will let you know when he has had enough. You can trust your baby to ask for exactly the "down time" he needs to develop properly. Watch your son, follow his cues, and enjoy watching him grow and develop.

My Baby Looks Uncomfortable!

I have just gotten a sling for my newborn son, and my baby seems to really like it. He falls right asleep, and I love the freedom. I have one concern though: he looks awfully squished in there to me. Is he really ok?

Remember that a full-term, healthy baby will let you know if he is uncomfortable. What may seem 'squished' to you may actually feel just right to him. After all, it was pretty tight quarters in the womb! This curled up position may be exactly what he is used to.

That said, it is always a good idea to observe basic safety precautions as you learn to wear your baby. Please review the Babywearing Safety section on page 88. Make certain baby has good airflow around his nose and mouth and that no circulation is cut off. If you live in a warm climate, make sure baby is not too hot in the sling. Slings keep babies toasty! Pre-term babies breathe easier in the upright position, so this would be a good position to start with if your baby is not full-term.

Newborn on my Back?

I keep hearing that I should not wear my baby on my back until she can hold her head up. She is only three weeks old, and I really want to wear her on my back. I like my sling, but I get so tired carrying all that weight in front. Is there any way I can wear my newborn on my back?

Absolutely! In fact you have several options for wearing your newborn on your back. She may enjoy reclining on your back in a sling in the fashion described on page 121, or she may enjoy being upright in one of the carriers that offers proper head and neck support for a newborn. Newborns often enjoy having their legs tucked up under them (the fetal position) when they are upright on your back. Wraparound carriers can be used safely to secure a newborn to your back, provided the fabric is pulled up high enough to fully support baby's head and neck. Fabric packs can also work well to support baby's head and neck in back. Fabric packs with a curved top design are especially suited for tiny babies (please see photo page 79). Plan to have another person help you get your baby situated as you are learning. Check her position often in a mirror.

The Reluctant Sling Baby

I have read about all the benefits of wearing my baby, and I really want to wear my baby girl, but when I put her in the sling, she just struggles and fusses and will not settle down. Has anyone else ever had a baby who just doesn't seem to like the sling?

Do not give up yet! Babywearing is a learned skill. Parents need to learn *and* babies need to learn. Many parents try to learn babywearing at the same time as their baby, leading to frustration for everyone. Although it may seem like your baby does not like the sling, what she may actually dislike is the process of being put in the sling. (You may want to review the Babywearing Tips section on page 85.) These simple tips may help: start with a well-fed, rested baby; do most of your adjusting and learning with the carrier before you pick her up; and get moving as soon as she is safely in the sling. *Go outside* for a walk as soon as baby is safely in the carrier. When my daughter was a newborn, we would load her in the sling on the porch and head off on a long, brisk walk immediately. Most babies cannot resist the outdoors!

Persistance pays off: try new carriers, new positions, and watch other babywearers. A favorite position for newborns is *upright*, with the head out, not tucked in and reclined, as is often shown in photos. Try one of the vertical carrying positions. A good place to start is the Newborn Nestle (page 113). Remember that many babies are struggling against the sensation of being restricted, and they may prefer positions that leave their head out and their feet and arms free.

If you are unsure as to which position to try with your baby, simply observe how she usually likes to be carried in your arms, then try to imitate that position with a carrier. For example, if you usually carry her upright over your shoulder, she will probably like the Newborn Nestle (page 113). If you usually carry her on your hip, try the Hip Carry (page 99).

It may also help to let an experienced babywearer wear *your* baby. Someone with more experience may be able to try several positions expertly and quickly and help find one that your baby likes. You can then imitate the favorite position. With persistence, you will find out what works best for you and your baby.

Babywearing and Breastfeeding

I love wearing my two-month-old daughter, but I am getting frustrated trying to breastfeed her while she is in the sling. I can latch her on pretty well, but when I try to move around, her mouth always slips off the breast, and it is painful! She gets frustrated, and I end up taking her out and nursing her. What am I doing wrong?

You are not alone. Many women report that it takes practice to be able to competently nurse a baby in a sling or other soft carrier. In fact, many babywearers consider nursing in a carrier while moving to be "advanced babywearing." The easiest way to begin to nurse in a carrier is to sit down. Loosen the carrier so you have some space to work with. Watch your baby the whole time so you can both get the hang of it. If you want to try moving while baby is nursing in the carrier: latch baby on then tighten the carrier and slowly start moving around, supporting baby's head with one hand so she stays firmly latched on. Rest assured: Breastfeeding while on the go gets easier as you both get the hang of it and as baby gets bigger and stronger. Do what works best for you and your daughter.

Babywearing During Pregnancy

I have a 16-month-old who weighs about 21 pounds and is not walking more than five steps at a time. I just found out that I am pregnant. Is it possible to continue to wear my toddler while I am pregnant?

In general, it is fine to continue to wear your baby throughout your pregnancy, but please check with your health care provider first. If your pregnancy is considered high risk, your health care provider may suggest more conservative guidelines.

That said, most pregnant women who have older children can and do end up carrying their older children at some point, often out of pure necessity. Plan to follow some commonsense guidelines: rest when you are tired, put your child down if you are in pain, and do not push yourself. You may have to experiment a bit to find carrying positions that are comfortable for you as your belly expands. Here are some positions that have worked for other pregnant moms: slinging baby on the side or back or using a wraparound or pack on the back and tying the waist strap either high above the belly or well below it. Pregnant mothers report liking the High Back Carry with a fabric pack as this method of tying avoids having straps across the belly. (See page 156 for a description of the High Back Carry.)

Babywearing and Sibling Rivalry

My second child is due any day now and I am worried that my first born will be jealous if I wear the new baby in "his" sling. I do not want babywearing to contribute to increased sibling rivalry.

Most parents find that their soft baby carrier becomes absolutely indispensable with the arrival of subsequent children. Keeping up with your older children is much easier when baby is secure in a soft carrier and you have two hands free. Many parents report that babywearing can actually *help* an older sibling with the transition of a new baby in the family.

> We have three children all spaced approximately three years apart. I wore my children until I was quite pregnant. I carried them as much as I could, while I could, as I knew it wouldn't be possible after the baby was born. When the baby was born, I wore the baby constantly. From the older sibling's point of view, baby was completely hidden and they easily forgot

that there was even a baby in there. I had two hands free at all times to give hugs, pick up the child, prepare lunch, help with the potty, etc. None of our children have had any issues with sibling transition at all. They've all become very used to the new little one immediately because I wore the baby all of the time and never said, "No I can't hold you now," or "No, mommy's holding the baby."

Tanya Westerman
Owner of Kangaroo Korner, LLC

You may want to consider purchasing a matching child-sized sling for your first-born child so he can carry his own "baby" while you are carrying yours (see the Appendix for resources for Child-Sized Slings). This helps the new older sibling feel like he is part of things.

Too Late to Try Babywearing?

I'd like to try wearing my baby, but my baby is 13 months old already. Is it too late to give babywearing a try?

Not at all. If your baby enjoys being held, you can find a way to use a soft baby carrier. The key to wearing an older baby is to make it fun! Try to distract baby from the "work" of getting settled in a carrier. Start with a very simple carrier (pouches are great for this purpose), try to slip baby in quickly and efficiently, and then start walking immediately. Talk to your baby the entire time about anything (except babywearing!). You may want to give your baby something to hold (a snack, a sippy cup of water, a small toy) while you are getting him settled. Once your baby is in the carrier, leave him be. Give him a chance to get used to the carrier while you stay in motion and point out interesting things. When he seems to have had enough of being held, help him out of the carrier immediately. Make each babywearing experience a positive one for your child and respect his wishes.

When your baby is comfortable with the babywearing procedure, it is fine to start experimenting with different positions and various carriers, even those with a more involved on/off. Many parents eventually prefer to carry their heavier babies and toddlers on their back. Remember the woven wraparound carriers distribute baby's weight the best over both your shoulders and waist, but the packs can be a bit easier to get on and off.

Books for Parents

- Allport S. 1997. *A Natural History of Parenting: From Emperor Penguins to Reluctant Ewes, a Naturalist Looks at How Parenting Differs in the Animal World and Ours.* New York: Harmony Books.
- Blurton Jones N., ed. 1972. *Ethnological Studies of Child Behavior.* Cambridge: Cambridge University Press.
- Bowlby J. 1990. *A Secure Base: Parent-Child Attachment and Healthy Human Development.* New York: Basic Books.
- Bowlby J. 1982. *Attachment.* 2nd edition. New York: Basic Books.
- DeLoache JS, Gottlieb A, eds. 2000. *A World of Babies: Imagined Childcare Guides for Seven Societies.* Cambridge: Cambridge University Press.
- Fontanel B. 1998 *Babies Celebrated.* New York: Harry N. Abrams, Inc.
- Heller S. *1997. The Vital Touch: How Intimate Contact with your Baby Leads to Happier, Healthier Development.* New York: Owl Books.
- Hunt J. 2001. *The Natural Child: Parenting from the Heart.* Gabriola Island, BC, Canada: New Society Publishers.
- Karp H. *2002. The Happiest Baby on the Block.* New York: Bantam Doubleday Dell.
- Lan YCL, Lin CL, Lin B. 2001. *Bonding via Baby Carriers: The Art & Soul of the Miao and Dong People.* Taipei, Taiwan: Les Enphants Co.
- Liedloff J. 1986. *The Continuum Concept.* Boulder: Perseus Publishing.
- Linden DW, et al. 2000. *Preemies: The Essential Guide for Parents of Premature Babies.* New York: Pocket Books.
- Luddington-Hoe SM, Golant SK. 1993. *Kangaroo Care: The Best You Can Do to Help Your Preterm Infant.* New York: Bantam Books.
- Mahler, MS, Pine F, Bergman A. 1975. *The Psychological Birth of the Human Infant: Symbiosis and Individuation.* New York: Basic Books.
- Reynolds J. 1996. *Mother and Child: Visions of Parenting from Indigenous Cultures.* Rochester: Inner Traditions International.
- Sears W, Sears M. 2001. *The Attachment Parenting Book: A Commonsense Guide to Understanding and Nurturing Your Baby.* Boston: Little Brown and Company.
- Sears W, Sears M. 1993. *The Baby Book: Everything You Need to Know About Your Baby from Birth to Age Two.* Boston: Little, Brown and Company.

- Sears W, Sears R, Sears J, Sears M. 2004. *The Premature Baby Book: Everything You Need to Know About Your Premature Baby from Birth to Age One.* Boston: Little, Brown and Company.
- Small M. 1999. *Our Babies, Ourselves: How Biology and Culture Shape the Way We Parent.* New York: Anchor Books.
- Steingraber S. 2001. *Having Faith: An Ecologist's Journey to Motherhood.* Boulder: Perseus Publishing.
- Taffel R, et al. 2002. *Parenting by Heart: How to Stay Connected to Your Child in a Disconnected World.* Boulder: Perseus Publishing.
- Witman A. 2003. *Babywearing and Baby Slings* (a booklet). Aneirin Press. www.users.adelphia.net/~seandonohue/babywearing/booklet.html

Books for Children

- Ashman L. 2003. *Babies on the Go.* San Diego: Harcourt, Inc.
- Bernhard E, Bernhard D. 1996. *A Ride on Mother's Back: A Day of Baby Carrying Around the World.* San Diego: Gulliver Books Harcourt Brace and Co.
- Cohen M. 1999. *Backpack Baby.* New York: Star Bright Books, Inc.
- Cohen M. 1999. *Mine! A Backpack Baby Story.* New York: Star Bright Books, Inc.
- Cohen M. 1999. *Say Hi, Backpack Baby.* New York: Star Bright Books, Inc.
- Cohen, M. 1999. *Wah-Wah! A Backpack Baby Story.* New York: Star Bright Books, Inc.
- Johnston E. 2004. *Dance With Me.* Available at: www.lulu.com/content/63423.
- Michels D. 2001. *Look What I See, Where Can I Be? In the Neighborhood.* Washington: Platypus Media, LLC.
- Morris A. 1989. *Hats, Hats, Hats.* New York: Lothrop, Lee and Shepard Books.
- Sears W, Sears M, Kelly CW. 2001. *What Baby Needs.* Boston: Little, Brown and Company.
- Stuve-Bodeen S. 1998. *Elizabeti's Doll.* New York: Lee and Low Books.

Articles

- Gross-Loh C. 2002. "Babywearing Tips." *Mothering.* 113, July/ August.
- Gross-Loh C. 2002. "Hold me close: The many advantages to wearing your baby." *Mothering.* 113:31-36, July/ August.
- Liedloff J. 1989. "The importance of the in-arms phase." *Mothering.* 50:17-19. Winter.
- Loyos A. 2004. "On the Day Sage Was Born." *Mothering.* 126:53-55, September/ October.
- Parker L. 2003. "Baby wearing: The importance of close physical proximity and touch. *API News: The Journal for Attachment Parenting Families.* 6(2):1-2. www.attachmentparenting.org
- Saines SB. 1990. "West African baby wearing – carrying your baby or toddler in a cloth." *Mothering.* 56, Summer.

Related Non-Profit Organizations

- **The Mamatoto Project, Inc.**
  Educates the general public on the advantages of babywearing and promotes the use of a simple piece of cloth as a traditional baby sling. How-to guides and videos www.mamatoto.org
- **The Rebozo Way Project**
  Dedicated to the encouragement of in-arms parenting.
  www.rebozoway.org   1-877-4REBOZO
- **Nine In, Nine Out (NINO)**
  Promotes babywearing. The name refers to the fact that babies are carried inside the womb for nine months and benefit greatly from being carried in a sling for at least the first nine months of life outside the womb.
  www.nineinnineout.org
- **Attachment Parenting International**
  Promotes parenting methods that create strong, healthy emotional bonds between children and their parents.
  www.attachmentparenting.org   1-615-298-4334
- **La Leche League, International**
  Provides information and support to women who choose to breastfeed.
  www.lalecheleague.org   1-800-LALECHE.

On-Line Resources

- **The BabyWearer.com**
  Fabulous, independent, on-line babywearing resource center: Consumer reviews, recommendations, active forum community, great articles, links, photos, and videos. A great place to start
  www.thebabywearer.com
- **Kangaroo Mother Care Promotions**
  Promotes Kangaroo Mother Care as the standard method of care for all newborn babies, both premature and full term
  www.kangaroomothercare.com
- **Yahoo Babywearing Group**
  Great online discussion group regarding babywearing in general. Many vendors are actively involved in this group and contribute feedback regarding design, wearing tips, and other insider information. Good source for information from experienced babywearers.
  www.groups.yahoo.com/group/babywearing
- **Peppermint.com**
  Traditional carriers from around the world
  Good quality wearing instructions and unique carriers for sale
  www.peppermint.com   1-866-737-7376
- **Kangaroo Korner**
  Babyslings: A hip full, not a handful
  Excellent wearing instructions and a variety of slings and pouches for sale
  www.kangarookorner.com   1-651-766-8337
- **TaylorMade Slings**
  Where babies belong
  Babywearing info and slings for sale
  www.taylormadeslings.com   1-480-895-2425
- **Mamma's Milk**
  Babywearing info, "celebrity slingers" and slings for sale
  www.mammasmilk.com   954-242-0257

The History of Babywearing in the U.S.

- Rayner Garner
  www.intuit.org.uk
- Sachi Yoshimoto
  www.enwrapture.org
- Dr. William Sears
  www.askdrsears.com

Ring Slings - Unpadded

- Maya Wrap
  www.mayawrap.com   1-888-MAYA WRAP
- ZoloWear
  www.zolowear.com   1-866-264-ZOLO
- Kangaroo Korner Unpadded Sling
  www.kangarookorner.com   1-651-766-8337
- TaylorMade Slings
  www.taylormadeslings.com   1-480-895-2425
- Rockin' Baby Sling
  www.rockinbabysling.com   1-888-645-BABY

Ring Slings - Fully Padded

- The Original Sears BabySling (NOJO)
  www.askdrsears.com   1-949-489-0020
- SlingEZee
  www.parentingconcepts.com   1-800-727-3683
- Over The Shoulder Baby Holder
  www.babyholder.com   1-800-637-9426

Ring Slings - Custom Padded/ Lightly Padded

- The Rosado Sling
  www.rosadosling.com   1-918-377-2282
- Kangaroo Korner
  www.kangarookorner.com   1-651-766-8337
- Moms in Mind Sarong Carrier
  www.momsinmind.com
  Matching baby clothes at Bumwear
  www.bumwear.com

Tie slings

- Rebozo
  www.rebozoway.org   1-877-4REBOZO

Pouches - Fixed

- New Native Baby Carrier
  www.newnativebaby.com   1-800-646-1682
- Chic Papoose, LLC
  www.chicpapoose.com
- Mamma's Milk Pouch
  www.mammasmilk.com
- Hotslings
  www.hotslings.com
- Kindersling
  www.kindersling.com   1-214-668-9803
- Gypsy Mama Towel Pouch
  www.gypsymama.com

Pouches - Adjustable

- Kangaroo Korner Adjustable Fleece or Cotton Pouch
  www.kangarookorner.com   1-651-766-8337
- Maya Wrap Pouch
  www.mayawrap.com   1-888-MAYA WRAP
- ZoloWear Pouch
  www.zolowear.com   1-866-264-ZOLO
- Mamma's Milk Invisibly Adjustable Pouch
  www.mammasmilk.com
- Sling Baby
  www.walkingrockfarm.com   1-866-635-2140

Pouches - Hybrid

- Wise Woman Sling
  www.wisewomansling.com   1-507-934-6012
- Baby Space Adjustable Pouch
  www.babyspaceslings.com

Hip slings

- HipHugger
  www.thehiphugger.com
- The Hip Hammock
  www.hiphammock.com   1-208-343-0016
- Hip Baby
  www.walkingrockfarm.com   1-866-635-2140
- RideOn Carrier
  www.rideoncarriers.com   1-866-874-3366

Wraparounds - Stretchy

- The Ultimate BabyWrap
  www.theultimatebabywrap.com   1-866-566-3720
- Moby Wrap
  www.mobywrap.com   1-888-879-1153
- The Baby Bundler
  www.babybundler.com   1-800-253-3502
- Hug-a-Bub
  www.hugabub.com   Australia +61 2 6685 5589
- The MamaBaby Sling
  www.mayawrap.com   1-888-MAYA WRAP

Wraparounds - Woven

- Didymos
  www.didymos.de   0 71 41/ 92 10 24
- Girasol
  www.peppermint.com   1-866-737-7376
- EllaRoo Baby Carrier
  www.peppermint.com   1-866-737-7376
- Gypsy Mama
  www.gypsymama.com
- Mama's Wings Wrap
  www.mamatoto.org
- Kabuki
  www.rosadosling.com   1-918-377-2282
- Extra long Rebozo
  www.rebozoway.org   1-877-4REBOZO
- The MamaRoo Baby Sling
  www.mamaroo.com

Fabric Packs

- Kozy Carrier
  www.kozycarrier.com
- Sachi Mei Tai
  www.sachicarriers.com
- Onbuhimo
  www.peppermint.com   1-866-737-7376
- Baby Back-Tie
  No longer available.
- Packababy
  www.packababy.com
- Mei Tai
  www.peppermint.com   1-866-737-7376

Constructed Packs

- The ERGO Baby Carrier
  www.ergobabycarrier.com   1-888-416-4888
- Baby Bjorn
  www.babybjorn.com   1-800-593-5522
- The Wilkinet Baby Carrier
  www.wilkinet.co.uk   +44 (0) 1239 841844
- Sutemi Pack
  www.sutemigear.com   1-866-444-BABY
- Weego Baby Carrier, Weego Preemie, Weego Twin
  www.weego.com
- BabyTrekker
  www.babytrekker.com   1-800-665-3957
- First Journey
  www.first-journey.com   1-800-665-3957

Back Torso Carriers

- Short Cloth Tying
  Buy breathable, resilient fabric (2 yards x 1 yard wide)
- LoveWrap Podaegi
  www.lovewrap.com
- EllaRoo Podaegi
  www.peppermint.com   1-866-737-7376
- FreeHand Podaegi
  www.freewebs.com/freehand
- FreeHand Hmong
  www.freewebs.com/freehand
- Baby Wrap
  www.babywrapinc.com   1-303-757-5564

Make Your Own Baby Carrier

- Simple Piece of Cloth
  A simple piece of cloth can be made into a *tie sling*, a *wraparound carrier*, or a *torso carrier*. Your fabric should be at least 25 inches wide (0.6 meters) and meet this criteria: mostly cotton, breathable, resilient, washable, has finished selvage (finished edges), and has a bit of diagonal give. The fabric *must not be too thick* or you will have trouble tying it. Cotton mesh fabric is wonderful. To test if a fabric is breathable, place over your nose and mouth and breathe normally. You need different lengths of fabric for different tying positions. A 2.8 yard length (2.6 meters) can be used by most people as a *tie sling*. If you plan on using all *wraparound* positions, choose 4.6 yards (4.2 meters) if you are up to 140 pounds and 5'8", 5 yards (4.6 meters) if you are up to 180 pounds and six feet, and 5.5 yards (5 meters) if you are above 180 pounds and over six feet. A shorter piece (about 2 x 1 yards, or 1.8 x 0.9 meters) may be used for a Short Cloth Tying *torso* carrier.

- On-Line Resources
  www.mamatoto.org
    Learn to make slings out of household items (sheets, shawls, etc) as well
    as strips of cloth
  www.jenrose.com
    Basic instructions for making several simple slings. Has techniques for
    using a bedsheet and making a tube-shaped sling.
  www.groups.yahoo.com/group/slingsewing
    Online community discuss do-it-yourself techniques for making many
    types of soft baby carriers
  www.thebabywearer.com
    Great sewing and improvising section with an active do-it-yourself
    forum
- Patterns for Ring Slings
  www.mayawrap.com 1-888-MAYA WRAP
  www.slingmemommy.com
  www.elizabethlee.com (complete kit)
- Where to Buy Sling Rings
  www.slingrings.com
- Patterns for a Pouch
  www.ida.net/users/stace/sling.html (fixed pouch)
  www.babyspaceslings.com/make1 (hybrid pouch)
- Patterns for a Tie Sling
  www.rebozoway.org

Child-Sized Slings

- TaylorMade Slings
  www.taylormadeslings.com 1-480-895-2425
- New Native Baby Carrier
  www.newnativebaby.com 1-800-646-1682
- Rebozo
  www.rebozoway.org 1-877-4REBOZO
- Maya Wrap
  www.mayawrap.com 1-888-MAYA WRAP

Doll Slings

- Magic Cabin
  www.magiccabin.com   1-888-623-3655
- Slings and More!
  www.slingsandmore.com
- Felix Pera Coat
  www.peppermint.com   1-866-737-7376
- Aiska Poncho
  www.peppermint.com   1-866-737-7376
- Mamaponcho
  www.mamaponcho.ch

Nursing Clothes

- Motherwear Catalog
  www.motherwear.com   1-800-950-2500

S